Lee de Forest
and the Fatherhood
of Radio

Lee de Forest
and the Fatherhood
of Radio

James A. Hijiya

Bethlehem: Lehigh University Press
London and Toronto: Associated University Presses

Associated University Presses
440 Forsgate Drive
Cranbury, NJ 08512

Associated University Presses
25 Sicilian Avenue
London WC1A 2QH, England

Associated University Presses
P.O. Box 39, Clarkson Pstl. Stn.
Mississauga, Ontario,
L5J 3X9 Canada

The paper used in this publication meets the requirements
of the American National Standard for Permanence of Paper
for Printed Library Materials Z39.48-1984.

Library of Congress Cataloging-in-Publication Data

Hijiya, James A.
    Lee de Forest and the fatherhood of radio / James A. Hijiya.
        p.   cm.
    Includes bibliographical references (p.   ) and index.
    ISBN 0-934223-23-8 (alk. paper)
    1. De Forest, Lee, 1873–1961.   2. Inventors—United States—
Biography.   3. Radio—United States—History.   I. Title.
621.38′092—dc20
    [B]   91-76959
                                                                   CIP

For
Barbara Jean Angela Najjar

A Note on Orthography

Lee de Forest learned to spell—but not to spell the way that everyone else did. Like his hero Thomas Edison, he ignored the conventions of orthography. To convey de Forest's habitual resistance to standard usage, this book will reproduce his words exactly as he wrote them, without relentlessly attaching an admonitory *sic*.

Contents

Acknowledgments

The written word is a private medium, and bookish people keep to themselves. The student with a paperback cradled on her crossed ankles as she sits in the park and ignores the frisbees whirring by, or the retired professor who spends all day in the twilight of a microfilm reader—they know that study requires solitude. To learn, you must be alone.

But, on the other hand:

I owe much to Michael Kammen. He suggested the De Forest family as a dissertation topic, supervised the initial research and writing, and later encouraged me as I resurrected John and Lee de Forest in separate books. He taught history as if it mattered, but not as if it were all that mattered. After Thanksgiving dinner, he offered me a cigar.

Many other friends and colleagues read this book in various stages of its seemingly interminable development. For generous criticisms I thank Glenn Altschuler, Shaleen Barnes, Michael Colacurcio, Clark Larsen, Betty Mitchell, Larry Moore, and John Werly. Bob Bento of the Physics Department at the University of Massachusetts Dartmouth tutored me in elementary electronics, and I also received valuable instruction from Bill Hwang and Barney Dennison. Bill Johnson translated Latin for me, while Kevin O'Brien escorted me through the dark labyrinths of the law library and patent law. Tom Lewis, who was finishing his masterly history of early radio, *Empire of the Air,* at the same time I was completing this biography, unselfishly shared his research with me. He allowed me to read and plunder his manuscript, sent me photocopies of newspaper clippings and other documents (particularly regarding Phonofilm), helped me obtain photographs, and offered all sorts of useful advice and entertaining information. Ellen DuBois graciously sent me newspaper clippings about Nora Blatch de Forest and the woman suffrage campaign of 1913.

The late Marie Mosquini de Forest granted me a useful and enjoyable interview at her home in Hemet, California; and Janice Price navigated me there from Los Angeles. Henry Fukai provided me with a place to stay in San Francisco when I was doing research near there; and Ed and Lauren Szymanoski did the same in Washington, DC. Rhoda Barney Jenkins permitted me to examine and publish photographs from her important collection on the woman suffrage movement. Her assistance to researchers is so generous that her house in Greenwich, Connecticut, has become practically a hostel for historians. Dorothy Owens and Cheryl Phillips typed early versions of the manuscript, then the University of Massachusetts Dartmouth lent me a computer so I could rewrite it and type it myself. I still needed Mrs. Phillips, however, to solve the mystery of the laser printer and to provide other sorts of clerical assistance.

Archivists and librarians played an essential role in the making of this book. Estelle McLaughlin of the De Forest Memorial Archives in 1975 when they were in Los Altos Hills, California, helped me locate not only the necessary documents but also a cheap motel, a convenient bus to the archives, and a bountiful supply of hot coffee. Shaleen Barnes and other librarians at U Mass Dartmouth used their mastery of computer networks to obtain important books and articles that I would never have been able to discover without the experts' assistance. I am indebted too to the staffs of the following institutions: Bancroft Library, University of California, Berkeley; Brown University Libraries, Providence, Rhode Island; the Cayuga Museum, Auburn, New York; Oral History Collection of Columbia University, New York; Cornell University Libraries, Ithaca, New York; Library of Congress, Washington; Archives Center, National Museum of American History, Smithsonian Institution, Washington; and Yale University Libraries, New Haven, Connecticut. Travel grants from the John Anson Kittredge Educational Foundation and the University of Massachusetts Dartmouth Foundation enabled me to travel to archives in New Haven, New York, Los Altos Hills, and Washington.

Rhoda Barney Jenkins, the Library of Congress, and the AT&T Archives reproduced photographs from their collections or permitted me to publish them. At the Perham Foundation, George Durfey searched for photographs in the De Forest Memorial Archives, Jim Weldon reproduced them, and Don Koijane granted me permission to publish them. I am also indebted to people whose expertise, constructiveness, and patience assisted in the publishing process: directors Stephen Cutcliffe and Philip Metzger of Lehigh University Press; the anonymous reviewer for Lehigh who recommended my manuscript for publication; and director Julien Yoseloff, managing editor Michael Koy, copy editor Deborah Mitchell, and production editor Regina Phair of Associated University Presses.

All these people and institutions remind me that no one can succeed—not even in so private an endeavor as writing—without the generous support of others. The scholar is more solitary than some people, but must nonetheless acknowledge an ever-expanding dependence on family, friends, and society.

This book is dedicated to Barbara Najjar, my wife. She did not assist with the research and writing. She did not type the manuscript, nor correct the proofs. She has her own work to do. She gave me welcome encouragement, but her main contribution to my work was to permit me long hours of solitude in my study. Barbara does not help me write books; she enriches my life in more important ways. So this book is dedicated, with love, to her.

Lee de Forest
and the Fatherhood
of Radio

Introduction: Lives of Great Men: 1890

Lee de Forest was an inventor. In 1906 he created the "Audion," the three-electrode vacuum tube, which became the foundation of the electronics industry for half a century. He was a pioneer in radio and talking pictures, and he worked on projects ranging from television to solar energy. Holder of more than three hundred patents, he was one of the most prolific inventors in American history.

But he was more than that. Lee de Forest had an immense curiosity that extended beyond science and engineering to politics, literature, religion. His active and far-ranging mind became a register for many social and intellectual events during his long life: from Populism to McCarthyism, and from Darwinism to agnosticism. But while his interests were diverse, his vision was not. For him invention was not merely a vocation, but a worldview. He represented a technological progressivism that advocated reform, but it was reform stemming less from social engineering than from real engineering. Although he favored certain improvements in law and education, he did not think that these would be the basis of social transformation. Instead, he believed that inventions—ranging from radios to war planes—would reform the human condition and that the future was more in the hands of inventors than statesmen. The millenium would be a technical innovation, with himself as one of its principal inventors.

De Forest was a loner. Growing up in the late nineteenth century, he admired men like Thomas Edison, who worked independently, directing their own research and producing inventions they could call their own. De Forest, however, was doomed to spend most of his life in the twentieth century, when invention was becoming a collective enterprise, conducted by gigantic corporations like AT&T with its battalions of engineers. Moreover, technology was becoming so complex, the process of invention so diffuse, that it was rare for one laboratory, much less one person, to be responsible for a major invention. Something as complicated as the radio was not produced by one person at a particular moment, but by many people making a series of inventions over decades. No individual could convincingly claim to be *the* inventor of radio, though de Forest would try his best. In the twentieth century, it became more difficult for an inventor to acquire the fame of a Morse, a Bell, or an Edison. Although Henry Ford might make his name a byword through his company's colossal success in manufacturing and sales, he could not do it through inventing alone. For Lee de Forest this growth of corporate inventing was a challenge that he resolutely faced and partially overcame. Only through individualistic efforts could he achieve his grandest objectives.

From childhood to old age, de Forest pursued fame. Indeed, that pursuit may have been the main motive for his career of invention. Of course, there were other motives: to make money, to serve humankind by providing it with useful machines, to have the intellectual satisfaction of solving problems and mastering the physical world. But de Forest's hunger for glory made itself evident so often and for so long that it overshadowed other drives. Always a loner, he had a hard time finding and keeping friends; never being popular, he sought to be famous. When he was inventing, or later when he was trying to make the world recognize him as "Father of Radio," he strove to make his mark in society, in history, and in eternity; to achieve some sort of justification.

Fame was a crucial goal, but it was just one step toward a higher one, immortality. As a young man, de Forest came to spurn conventional notions of an immortal soul; but he never ceased to seek ways to overcome death—not merely physical death but also the spiritual death of living without purpose. The fame of his inventions would, he hoped, keep his memory forever alive. Moreover, the good that his inventions did for humanity—their contribution to progress—would give meaning to his existence. By helping to build the future, he would become an indelible part of it. For Lee de Forest, invention was a substitute for religion.

This book is not primarily an analysis of de Forest's contribution to technology—readers seeking that will find it in the volumes by Hugh G. J. Aitken and Gerald F. J. Tyne, each of which is definitive in its field.[1] Instead this book is the chronicle of a spiritual quest. Lee de Forest was an important inventor, and this biography explains what moved him to become one. It shows how de Forest's devotion to invention was part of his search, in a universe from which deity had disappeared, for a new kind of light. The book is not a study in the history of technology but in the history of the religion of technology.

Lee de Forest grew up in the midst of an international debate over what historian Charles Cashdollar has called "positivism." A. J. Balfour, the English politician and philosopher, described positivism in 1888 as "that general habit or scheme of thought which, on its negative side, refuses all belief in anything beyond phenomena and the laws connecting them, and on its positive side attempts to find in the 'worship of humanity,' or, as some more soberly phrase it, in 'the service of man,' a form of religion unpolluted by any element of the supernatural." De Forest and many of his fellow inventors in the electronics field—his heroes and his rivals—exemplified this positivist impulse in varying degrees.[2]

Nearly all were either forthrightly skeptical or, if still keeping the faith, doing so in the most tenuous or heterodox fashion. The agnostic Alexander Graham Bell confessed to his future bride that he knew nothing of "Salvation, Faith and all other points of theoretical religion." Thomas Edison denied the existence of a personal god and deplored the "incurably religious" attitude of most people. Nikola Tesla, who would become famous by inventing systems for generating and transmitting electricity, was the grandson, son, and nephew of Serbian Orthodox priests. However, he rebelled against his parents by rejecting a clerical vocation; denied the existence of the spirit; explained all phenomena in terms of matter and energy; claimed that the human being was a perfect automaton, a "meat machine," responding to external stimuli and possessing no free will; and pioneered in the science of robotics.[3]

British physicist Oliver Lodge, the grandson and nephew of clergymen, said he "emerged out of the slight hold evangelism had upon me into a pleasant but far from irreverent breadth"—a capacious breadth that encompassed spiritualism. Michael Pupin, professor of engineering at Columbia University, attended Henry Ward Beecher's church because of that preacher's avoidance of dogma and his "gospel of humanity." Guglielmo Marconi wore his religion as lightly as his marriage vows. Baptized as a Catholic but raised as a Protestant, he married a Protestant, but returned to Catholicism when he decided to marry a beautiful young woman from the Vatican nobility. His daughter by his first wife recalled that, because "in recent years he had actively practiced no religion," he was "easily persuaded that he might find inner peace and greater harmony with Cristina if he embraced Catholicism." E. Howard Armstrong, pioneer of high-fidelity music and FM radio, had religious parents but showed no sign of their influence by the time he was in high school. One exception to the rule of inventors as doubters and an apparent opponent of positivism was J. Ambrose Fleming, inventor of the Fleming Valve, who read his Bible daily and preached on the evidence of the Resurrection. Even Fleming, however, had to adjust his religion to accord with his science, noting that each enterprise had to take into account the valid conclusions reached by the other.[4]

If agnosticism was the negative side of positivism, the other side was the gospel of humanity. The "electricians" (as electrical inventors were called at the turn of this century) derived a sense of purpose from the belief that their work improved human welfare. Declaring that invention was the most important product of the human brain, Tesla said that inventing's "ultimate purpose is the complete mastery of mind over the material world, the harnessing of the forces of nature to human needs." Tesla claimed to have conceived the idea of the alternating-current motor while reciting from Goethe's *Faust,* and he was not the only inventor who wanted to use seemingly diabolical magic to turn earth into paradise. Edison, the "Wizard of Menlo Park," had this as his motto: "Work—bringing out the secrets of nature and applying them for the happiness of man." After a wireless SOS made possible the rescue of some of the passengers on the *Titanic,* the thankful survivors presented Marconi with a gold medal, and he said he "felt gratitude that wireless telegraphy has again helped to save human lives."[5]

Besides inventing, the electricians served humanity through other activities, sometimes even through ones that interfered with their careers as inventors. Bell used much of the money he made from the telephone and the phonograph to subsidize his principal life's work, teaching the deaf. When he started a school for the deaf, he said, "I can be of far more use as a teacher of the deaf than I can ever be as an electrician." While Ambrose Fleming lived, he supported Christian missionary work in London; when he died, he left most of his estate to charities that dispensed both spiritual and material succor to the poor. Even Marconi, whose twin preoccupations were wireless and women, served mankind after a fashion by undertaking numerous diplomatic missions on behalf of the Italian government. However much one might doubt the humanitarian value of working as an apologist for Benito Mussolini, there is no need to question Marconi's earnest desire to serve his native land.[6]

But if humanitarianism went hand-in-hand with agnosticism, so too did a third common characteristic of the electrical inventors;

namely, an extraordinary craving for extraordinary achievement. When Bell was nineteen years old, his brother observed "your wish to do something great"; and after the first public demonstration of the telephone, the inventor noted happily that "My name is sure now to be well-known to all scientific men." When Tesla considered entering a prize competition for extraterrestrial communication, he wrote that the money award was a "trifling consideration, but for the great historical honor of being the first to achieve this miracle I would be almost willing to give my life." Marconi was money-minded enough to protest that "A man cannot live on glory alone," but he also knew that glory was one thing making life worth living. "The principal driving force of Marconi's life," according to biographer W. P. Jolly, "had been the ambition to cover the world with a wireless system of his own and to found a great company to manage and exploit that system." Marconi achieved all that but still was tormented by a relentless hunger for greatness. In middle age, long after his fabulous youthful success in wireless, he confessed repeatedly to his wife that his creativity was exhausted and that he no longer wanted to live. Marconi always managed to rally from his gloom, but not every inventor was so fortunate. Howard Armstrong brought suits in the courts and wrote letters to editors, trying to convince the world of his achievements. Squandering his time, money, and energy on litigation instead of invention, he grew despondent in the belief that his days as an inventor were over. So he killed himself. Afterwards an acquaintance recalled that Armstrong's obsession with himself and his inventions had made him "unnatural" and nearly mad. "What price glory?" wondered the acquaintance.[7]

Glory was a purchase on immortality, and the pursuit of immortality was one of the forces driving the process of invention. Michael Pupin gave Marconi "praise that is almost beyond words" by saying that Marconi had taught wireless telegraphy to the world and that his work would live on even after his death. "And that means his work is immortal," said Pupin, a notable inventor in his own right. "It is the greatest thing that can be said of a man's work." When Bell's telephone won a gold medal at an exposition, he said that gold was far less durable than the achievement itself, which would last as long as history. Tesla maintained that it was impossible for others to understand the inspiration for further research that he gained from knowing that his inventions had become "a matter of history." Tesla's work was largely funded by J. P. Morgan, the financier who had created General Electric,

AT&T, International Harvester, and US Steel. But during an argument the inventor did not hesitate to tell the capitalist: "You are a big man but your work is wrought in passing form. Mine is immortal."[8]

Pupin, Marconi, Bell, Tesla, and the others[9] believed that they were building a better world, making permanent improvements in the human condition, and thereby overcoming their own deaths. In a universe from which God had disappeared, the inventors thought that their contributions to civilization would give them life everlasting. Lee de Forest, a man on a religious quest, traveled in good and plentiful company.

In 1890, seventeen-year-old Lee de Forest wrote a letter to his father. "Dear Sir," he began, "Will you favor me with your ears for a few moments?" After explaining that he intended to become a "machinest and inventor, because I have great talents in that direction," he said he wished to attend the Sheffield Scientific School at Yale University. Lee knew that this choice would not please his father, who wanted him to go to Yale College rather than Sheffield and to prepare for the ministry rather than for inventing. "I write this," the boy assured his father, "with no ill will in the least."

As befitted someone who wanted to be a "machinest," Lee produced this message on a recent invention, the typewriter. But before giving the letter to his father, he turned it over and added a note for his mother, which included verses from Henry Wadsworth Longfellow's "A Psalm of Life":

> Lives of great men all remind us
> We can make our lives sublime,
> And departing, leave behind us
> *Footprints on the sands of time.*
> Footprints that perhaps another,
> Traveling o'er life's desert plain,
> A forlorn and ship-wrecked brother,
> Seeing may take heart again.

"I want to leave footprints on the sands of time," wrote the ambitious boy. "I can do so best by takeing the scientific course. Don't you think so?"[10]

Because Lee altered several of Longfellow's lines, it is likely that he quoted from memory; apparently he considered the poem important enough to merit memorization. Written when Longfellow was rallying from one of his frequent states of depression, "A Psalm of Life" denies the gloomy suspicion that "Life is but an empty dream" and affirms instead that "Life is real!" Rejecting both meditation on the "dead Past" and fruitless imagining of the Future, it urges one to be "up and doing" and to "Act,—act in the living Present!" One's "destined end or way," says Longfellow, is "to act, that each tomorrow / Find us farther than to-day."[11]

"A Psalm of Life" nicely summarizes the philosophy of Lee de Forest. Like Longfellow, he often plunged into depression and had to exhort himself out of it. He, too, found relief through action, and like the poet he could not tell whether action—moving farther each day—was an "end" or a "way." Both Longfellow and de Forest believed that they could make their lives sublime and that their footsteps would somehow be preserved in the ever-shifting sands of time.[12]

1

An Enduring Record for Fame: 1893

Lee de Forest was born in a parsonage. For someone who would later become an apostle of science and agnosticism, this fact was not without significance. His mother, the former Anna Robbins (1848–1927), had spent her youth in Muscatine, Iowa, where her father was pastor of the Congregational Church. Graduating from Iowa College (later renamed Grinnell) in 1868, she married the Rev. Henry Swift De Forest[1] a year later. De Forest (1833–1896) had ancestors who had come to New York and Connecticut in the seventeenth century. He did not, however, have money. As the only one of four brothers to attend college, he made his way through Yale College and Divinity School with the aid of a scholarship founded by a distant relative. Taking years off to earn money as a tutor—and as a chaplain in the Union Army during the Civil War—he did not receive his first pastorate until 1866, thirteen years after matriculating at Yale. From then until 1878 he served Congregational churches in Des Moines, Council Bluffs, and Waterloo, Iowa. After a year as financial secretary of Iowa College, he was appointed president of Talladega College in Alabama, a school established by the Freedmen's Bureau and the American Missionary Association in 1867 to educate recently emancipated blacks. Taking the post in 1879, he remained there until his death. Anna and Henry De Forest had three children. The eldest, Mary, was born in 1871; the youngest, Charles Mills, in 1878; the middle child, Lee, was born on 26 August 1873, in the parsonage of the First Congregational Church of Council Bluffs, Iowa.[2]

Lee seems to have been fond of his mother: in his autobiography he recalled "the sweetness of her character" and "her loving tenderness." When he was undergoing hard times in 1907, he was grateful for the "love & confidence & aid" she gave him; in 1926 he said he had written her every Sunday since he had left home; he visited her for two weeks in 1927 when she was nearing death; and in his later years he always placed her picture on his bedside table. Yet his journals, letters, and autobiography convey very little specific information about her. As a result, she seems a shadow in the background of his life—as he put it, a "sainted presence."[3]

The same cannot be said of his father. A very palpable presence, Henry De Forest was not only a parent to be loved but also a hero to be admired, a leader to be followed, and an opponent to be fought. The Rev. Mr. De Forest played no obscure role in the life of his son.

Henry De Forest set an example of human service that Lee would strive, however imperfectly, to follow. For instance, when Henry was drafted into the Union army in 1863, his classmates at Yale offered to pay three hundred dollars for a substitute for him. De Forest, however, refused the offer, saying that his duty to his country was a debt no substitute could pay. Similarly, the minister later viewed the presidency of Talladega College as a "sacred duty" and an "unsurpassed opportunity for influencing men." When he died, his tombstone bore this epitaph: "He lived for others." Although hardly an agnostic like most of the inventors

DR. De FOREST   MRS. De FOREST

Henry and Anna De Forest. Lee's father gave him a heroic example of zeal and service; his mother gave him consolation. Photos from obituary of Anna De Forest in *American Missionary* **magazine (1927), courtesy of United Church Board for World Ministries.**

whose number his son would soon join, Rev. De Forest shared their dedication to "the service of man." Lee de Forest felt more than a little pressure to become a benefactor of mankind, like his father.[4]

Although pastor of a Christian flock, Henry De Forest was a shepherd along the lines of giant-killing David. Never shrinking from any form of combat, he often told his children about his exploits in the War Between the States, particularly about one battle in which he gathered canteens, filled them with water, carried them across a field of fire, and distributed them to cheering Union troops. Seeking to inculcate equal courage and stamina in his sons, he urged them to remember their ancestor Gideon De Forest, a veteran of the American Revolution, as well as the warlike Gideon of the Bible. "May both of my Boys be stalwarts," he wrote in a letter, "regular Gideonites of the tribe of De Forests. No weak-kneed, faint-hearted, namby pamby among my male successors. Only two, but each a lion."[5]

For chaplain De Forest, the Civil War was a holy war. After seeing President Lincoln and a retinue of jubilant freedmen triumphantly enter Richmond in April 1865, De Forest announced that "Nemesis is satisfied. Even handed justice is finding the scalebeam horizontal." But freeing the slaves did not fully achieve justice; only *educating* them would do that. Regarding his work at Talladega College as a continuation of the Civil War, he said:

> I am glad I was in that fight [the war] and am in this. This is the longer, and we are not beyond Gettysburg. I shall never see our Appomattox; but some one will; and it may be said of me one day, "He fought a fairly decent fight."[6]

The analogy between school teaching and war was not grossly hyperbolic. In 1870, a year of "Ku Klux Riots" throughout the South, a gang of Klansmen marched from the Talladega courthouse to the campus and halted only when prominent townsmen persuaded them to turn back. That same year, an Irish-Canadian minister teaching blacks in a nearby town was lynched by a white mob, and his funeral was held at the college. The American Missionary Association sent rifles to Talladega, and in 1871 faculty members and students spent their nights standing guard over their school. Although white hostility toward the college had moderated by the time De Forest became president in 1879, it had not disappeared. In 1886 the mayor of Talladega called the college "a refuge for Northern reprobates, thieves, and incendi-

aries." President De Forest later said that if he were to write about
the college for a magazine, the article would have to be not only
temperate but also anonymous, lest it stir up wrath against the
school. "The South is full of fire and gunpowder," he said, and he
feared agitation and violence. When Henry De Forest took over
the Talladega College presidency, he was indeed picking up where
the Civil War left off.[7]

Militant as an Old Testament king when engaged in a holy
cause, De Forest had difficulty remembering that not every action
of his was graced with divine sanction. A man whose face showed
the determination, the absolute purpose, of a hanging-judge or a
bird of prey, De Forest could not tolerate opposition to his decisions and pronouncements. A fellow minister said that De Forest
was "characterized by an intense earnestness in his convictions
and by positive judgments. It was difficult for him at times to see
through other people's eyes." The Talladega College treasurer
also noted the president's "intense earnestness," which was evident in the tone of his voice and the flash of his eye, adding that
"he was not easily turned aside from a self-prescribed course."
Under De Forest, Talladega College had rigid rules governing
every aspect of a student's life, and those rules were strictly en-
forced. In 1889 and 1895, individual students were punished so
severely that the student body as a whole rose up in protest.[8]

Henry De Forest could not brook any sort of disorder. Every
book and paper on his desk was kept exactly in its appointed
place. When he marched across the Talladega campus, he would
stoop to pick up sticks and stones that had fallen into the path. He
walked stiffly upright, with shoulders thrown back militarily, and
taught his sons to do the same. Perhaps it was this fastidiousness,
this starchiness, that induced some of the students to refer to their
president as "Old Man Dee."[9]

There was something cold about De Forest, something
strangely detached. One day when he was writing in his study,
there was a commotion outside. His younger son, Charles, had
been thrown from a horse and carried home unconscious. As the
boy lay near death and everyone waited anxiously for the doctor
to arrive, De Forest resumed his writing. As Lee later recalled, "I
was never able to understand this calm indifference." It was several days before Charles regained his senses.[10]

Despite the peculiar godliness of his father, Lee de Forest had a
childhood not entirely unlike that of other boys in Talladega
(population 1,233 in 1880). On a typical morning he would build a
fire, say prayers, do chores, feed the horse, and go to school; in

Lee de Forest, ca. 1877. This picture was taken in Waterloo, Iowa, where de Forest lived until he was five. Photo courtesy of Perham Foundation.

the afternoon, play football, practice the cornet, and chop kindling; at night, study schoolwork and the Bible. He had a pet pig (Porcus) and calf (Augustus Caesar); he went fishing in a creek; he shot sparrows with a rifle and set off firecrackers on the Fourth of July.[11]

But in some ways Lee differed from the boys around him. While they were content to read juvenile fiction, he moved on to more engrossing literature, like the *Patent Office Gazette*. Ever since he had seen an Edison phonograph, Lee had been fascinated by technology. Clocks, printing presses, lawn mowers, plows—all sorts of machinery delighted him. After visiting an iron works, he built a miniature blast furnace out of an ashcan and an antique bellows (to his parents' dismay, he accidentally burned the nozzle off the heirloom); after examining a railroad train, he astonished his playmates by transforming packing crates and sugar barrels into a boy-sized locomotive that did everything but move. Not limiting himself to machines that he saw with his own eyes, he built replicas of ones he read about: the *Monitor* and the *Merrimac,* a castle with moat and drawbridge, and Ben Hur's chariot (pulled and later demolished by a recalcitrant yearling steer).[12]

At an early age he tried his hand at invention, but not always with positive results. On one occasion he gathered various brushes from around the house and experimented to see if they would serve as the reaping elements in a cotton-picking machine. The brushes successfully tore the cotton from the plants; unfortunately, however, Lee could not think of a way to remove the cotton from the brushes, except for the family to pick the tenacious white fluff from the bristles by hand. Undaunted by failures in humble projects, the nascent inventor tried the impossible. Once he designed a perpetual motion machine and wrote beneath his drawing of it, "I am actually amazed that I, a mere youth of 13 years, by my inventive genius and concentrated thought and study have succeeded where illustrious philosophers in times past have failed." This would be characteristic of Lee de Forest for the rest of his life: the hope and desire to do something great, the effort to do it, and the insistence that he had done it. His genius and determination would give his ambition—or even his wishful thinking—a kind of grandeur.[13]

Lee applied his concentrated thought and study not only to engineering but also to languages and letters. Talladega College, unlike Booker T. Washington's Tuskegee Institute, stressed the liberal arts more than the industrial ones. Reversing the policy of his predecessor, who had tried to change Talladega into an agricultural and mechanical school, President De Forest insisted that "they are sorry friends who tell you that industrial training is enough for the Negro." Anticipating W. E. B. Du Bois's later call for liberal education for the "talented tenth" of blacks, De Forest proclaimed that "while all should have the lower education, a great many should receive the higher." This emphasis on liberal arts was typical of schools sponsored by missionary associations. Indeed, it was one of De Forest's fellow leaders in the mission movement, Henry L. Morehouse of the American Baptist Education Society, who in 1896 coined the phrase "talented tenth," which Du Bois would later make his own.[14]

Since President De Forest insisted on the full range of liberal arts for students at Talladega, he surely would not allow his own son to get by with a narrowly technical education. In coming years the choice between liberal and professional educations would cause strife between father and son, but for now Lee complied with his father's wishes. Sitting in class alongside black students in the college preparatory course, he studied the same subjects as they did. Although he revolted against the study of "dead" languages ("nasty old Greek—Dogone it anyhow!"), he relished English and American literature. As a child he read Hawthorne's *Tanglewood Tales*, Lamb's *Tales from Shakespeare*, and every word of Cooper's Leatherstocking series. About 1891 he kept a commonplace book in which he copied favorite quotations from authors: Chaucer, Shakespeare, Dickens, and Leigh Hunt; Bradstreet, Poe, and Felicia Hemans; Jeremy Taylor; Newton and Locke; Franklin (Poor Richard), Paine, John Dickinson, Daniel Webster, and Lincoln.[15]

Early in life Lee resolved to read good books—"never trashy literature"—and to write well. After being thrilled by William H. Prescott's *The Conquest of Peru*, he swore off dime novels forever. Henceforth, he would read only morally inspiring fiction such as *Tom Brown at Rugby* and the stories in *The Youth's Companion*. In 1891 he began keeping a journal—which he continued, albeit sporadically, for more than half a century—to improve the clarity of his thought and writing. Throughout his life he wrote poetry, his earliest extant attempt being an ode commemorating his graduation from short pants to long. In 1890 he parodied Tennyson, one of his favorite authors, by composing *"Break, Break, Break. The dishwashing girl's lament."* When he left home in 1891, he was working on a never-completed novel, "Talzec, the Cliff King."[16]

With his literary interests and scientific abilities, Lee stood out from the other boys at Talladega—a fact not lost on Lee himself. He considered his black neighbors the intellectual equals of cattle, and he enjoyed showing to white boys the machines he had constructed, as examples of the superior Yankee genius. Such boastfulness did not endear him to the natives. He often had rock fights with the "nasty little rebs"; on one occasion a mob of white boys armed with sticks attacked him, but he took refuge among a crowd of "good nigs." Not all Negroes, however, were good Negroes. Some added to Lee's sense of persecution. When he was seventeen, Lee and his brother were coming home after fishing when they confronted "the meanest nigger devil I ever saw." The black took away their fish, held a rock to Lee's chest, and threatened to beat him. After the white boys pleaded for mercy, the black said that he would give them back their fish if they would give him a fishhook. Charles quickly produced one; and the black let them go, after forcing them to bid him good evening and forbidding them ever to return. ("Darned durned devil," wrote the humiliated Lee in his diary, "I will.")[17]

Lee seemed to spend his whole childhood at war with his neighbors, a war in which he lost every battle. One bully repeatedly terrified Lee by threatening to cut off his ears, ears that stood out like wings on the puny but loud-mouthed preacher's kid. Lee was beaten up by other boys so often that he acquired the nickname "Leago," derived from his desperate cry "Lea' go of me, lea' go of me." Constantly scrapping with both "scrub fool rebs" and "rough ignorant vicious niggers," Lee had few friends in Talladega.[18]

Nor was home a refuge. Lee and his brother were engaged in continual conflict. "It seemed to me in my childish pride," Lee later recalled, "that Charles lost no opportunity to taunt and tease me." Once, as Lee pounded nails in the cellar of their house, he struck his thumb. When Charles burst into laughter, Lee hurled the hammer at him but missed. Although nearly five years older than Charles, Lee was sufficiently undersized to make it a tolerably even fight. In March 1891, when Lee was seventeen and Charles twelve, "we pounded each other." A month later "he hit me on the jaw with a rock & I cau[gh]t him & slapped his head good—sad affairs. We boys are always quarreling."[19]

If combat with his neighbors and his brother were not enough to make Lee feel that life was war, there was always the antagonism with his father. To Henry De Forest fell responsibility for disciplining his children, and he was no man to shirk responsibility. Insisting on "firm rules and strict discipline, accompanied before and after with prayer," he took no risk of spoiling the child by sparing the rod. Lee was convinced that his father "erred on the side of severity," and the boy resisted whippings that he thought were undeserved (and there were many). Out in the proverbial woodshed, he defied his father as long as possible, withstanding "terrific wallops before I would concede a yell." While brother Charles howled at the first opportunity and thus escaped much punishment, Lee (as he recalled it later) was less willing to be bullied into obedience. Henry De Forest's strongmindedness reappeared in his first son.[20]

Not that Lee always bore his sorrows with stoical grace. Sometimes, after a spanking, he would run to his mother, crying, "I'm an adopted child or you wouldn't let me get beat so hard!" Often he crept down into the cellar, to a favorite spot that he called "the dark place," where he brooded in solitude on the misfortunes and injustices of life. Trying in vain to gulp down a lump in his throat, produced by shame and indignation, he sobbed for hours; sometimes he wished he were dead. But then he would overcome his "absolute despair," renew his courage, emerge from "the dark place," and return to the struggle of life.[21]

It was a pattern of behavior that would persist. Not just in childhood but all through his life, Lee de Forest sank deep into gloom. In 1906, while brooding over "dead hopes," he feared that he would go mad. A decade later he felt like "a dead man alive" because of frustrations in "the struggle for success against great odds"; in 1921 he noticed in himself "some strange physical deterioration, feeding in disappointment." Ensconced in the "dark place" that he always carried with him, he often suspected that life was but an empty dream. But then, when he approached despair, he would force himself out of depression by exhorting himself to "Act—act in the living Present" (as Longfellow had advised). Time and again Lee saved himself through the power of will.[22]

Lee dreaded and resented his father, and sometimes rebelled against him; but he also accorded him no small quantity of respect. The boy clipped out passages of letters from Henry Swift De Forest and pasted them in his journal, and he claimed to have learned from his father such virtues as "resolute determination" and "unfaltering faith in myself" and "a deep sense of duty, although our interpretations of duty differed." Moreover, despite the fierce and frequent conflict between father and son, there also were moments of genuine affection. Although usually stern, Rev. De Forest possessed a sense of humor that sometimes showed itself in an explosive, ringing laugh, an infectious laugh in which Lee often shared. Rev. De Forest could be tender, as on cold Saturday nights when Lee, after his weekly bath, warmed his toes before the fire while sitting in his father's lap. Then the minister spoke softly of events of the past week, sometimes giving a gentle reproof for misconduct but ending with a kiss.[23]

One of the happier experiences of Lee's youth was a journey to Colorado that he took with his father in the summer of 1889. Crossing the "Great American Desert" (which, he discovered, was "very sandy"), the sixteen-year-old marveled at prairie dog towns and giant ant hills. Taking a horseback ride, "we went a-tearing along, papa in his shirt sleeves & yelling like a Talladega drunk come Christmas time." Lee had never before seen his father "act so like a wild Indian." Together, man and boy climbed Pike's Peak.

For the rest of his life, Lee de Forest would delight in standing at the top of a mountain.[24]

At Colorado Springs, Lee visited the grave of writer and reformer Helen Hunt Jackson. Carving his initials into a tree near the grave, he placed himself before the eyes of posterity. To pay further tribute to "my comradess in poetry," he composed a ditty which began as follows:

> Stranger, pause and drop a tear.
> Helen Hunt lies buried here.
> She, whose pen the World *in*spired,
> Like all mortals has *ex*pired.[25]

The Muses visited Lee often on this western trip. Once when he asked for a bag of popcorn, his father promised to buy one if Lee would produce a verse suited to the occasion. The boy responded with a "Eulogy on Pop Corn." Even his letters home showed some deliberate craftsmanship, playfully imitating the dialect of either his neighbors in Alabama or characters in local-color fiction. He and his father had intended to examine a mine, he wrote, "but after we had supped we sot round with the miners & gassed away" and decided to postpone the adventure "cause Papa lowed as how he didn't wanter go into a mine."[26]

Before the garrulous fellowship of the miners got to him, Henry De Forest may have wanted to go underground in search of minerals. Although dissuaded from this excursion, he tried to add to his rock collection in a less inconvenient way, by asking another minister for specimens. Geology was not De Forest's only scientific interest. He maintained a lifelong enthusiasm for astronomy, and he was a member of the American Association for the Advancement of Science.[27]

Given this background, it is no surprise that he encouraged his son's curiosity about the natural world and took pride in the boy's accomplishments. But when Lee as a teenager proposed to devote his life to inventing, the father firmly said no. A hobby was one thing; a career, quite another. The Rev. Mr. De Forest had always hoped that his firstborn son would follow in his footsteps. On the day of Lee's birth, Henry De Forest penned a letter to his own mother. "I have desired," he wrote, "that if God so will, Anna, the daughter & wife of a minister, may be also the mother of a minister." As the years slipped away, De Forest's resolve did not. As a man not given to doubt his own judgment or to change his mind, he argued "long and prayerfully" with his son over the matter of vocation.[28]

By the time Lee was seventeen, the problem became a crisis, because he had to begin preparing for college. His father wanted him to study classical subjects in order to qualify for Yale College; Lee wanted to pursue engineering in order to gain entry to Sheffield Scientific School. In October 1890 Lee wrote the letter to his father in which he expressed his aspiration to leave footprints on the sands of time by becoming a great inventor. Four months later he sought the assistance of Thomas Edison. Forging his father's signature at the bottom of a letter, he asked Edison what a man should do with a son who wanted to study engineering. Lee hoped that Edison (a rebel against his own father) would write to Henry De Forest, urging that the boy be allowed to do as he pleased. However, Edison stayed out of this family quarrel by failing to reply, and the clash of wills between father and son persisted.[29]

Lee finally won. When his father realized that Lee was so determined to become an engineer that he would forego Yale entirely rather than follow the classical course, the minister reluctantly agreed to allow his son to prepare for the Scientific School at Yale. Nevertheless, the elder De Forest may not have given up entirely. The preparatory school to which he sent Lee was Mount Hermon in northwestern Massachusetts, a school founded and directed by the revivalist Dwight Moody. Perhaps De Forest still hoped for a change of heart in his stiff-necked son.[30]

When Lee left Talladega in the summer of 1891, he must have done so with a sense of relief. At last he could escape "the Rebs and Nigs" who so tormented him. He would get away from his quarrelsome brother and his even more troublesome father. By going North, it seemed, he would leave all these struggles behind.[31]

Traveling by sea to Boston, where he arrived on 16 July, he spent the rest of the summer at a natural history camp near Worcester. The camp, organized on a military basis complete with drills and inspections, provided more discipline than Lee could endure. Moreover, his lifelong penchant for practical jokes made him unpopular with his fellow cadets as well as with the camp's staff. During the single month of August he covered a toilet seat with pitch; swiped doughnuts from the mess hall (and was found out); threw moss at sleepers during the night; poured water on another camper's head ("and he, the big slob, reported"); stole clay pigeons from the shooting range and dropped them off the

Sketch made at summer camp, 1891. This scene of massacre may express de Forest's general hostility and aggression, his particular fear and disdain for blacks, or just the violent daydreams of the average American boy. Photo courtesy of Perham Foundation.

wharf to dive for them; placed one chair atop an electric light pole, and ran another up the flagpole. Apprehended by the camp director after the last escapade, Lee freely gave the names of the other boys involved. "Any one in my fix would have done it," he explained to himself, "especially if he had been only a few weeks with the other boys & didn't know how squeeling was regarded." During that month Lee got into two fights and barely avoided a third.[32]

On 1 September Henry De Forest, who was on one of his frequent fund-raising trips to the North, picked Lee up at camp and took him on the train to Mount Hermon. After two days helping the boy get settled, De Forest left him to grow and thrive in the new environment. Lee grew, to a height of five feet eleven inches. But thrive he did not. Although eighteen years old when he started prep school—older than most freshmen—he was awed by the mature, muscular farm boys there. "Such a lot of men— most of them big & grown," he reflected on the day of his arrival. "I'll never get acquainted." After a hard second day, he felt like crying.[33]

One reason why he felt insecure was his Southern upbringing. Reared among poor blacks, Lee feared that he had come to imitate them in speech and manners. When he first went North, he felt like a barbarian. This sense of inferiority, however, left him within a month and was replaced by a very different feeling. Finding that most of his fellow students were at Mount Hermon more for religious than intellectual reasons, he regretted that there were so many "hayseeds, farmers, ignorant, uncouth, rough fellows" there. For their part, the agrarians returned the sentiment. One of them gave Lee a new nickname, "Monkey-Face," and Lee was forced to admit that he was not popular. As at Talladega, he had his share of humiliations. Once, during an Easter vacation, he thought he had received an invitation to stay at the home of a fellow student. Arriving there, he found the other boy out of town and his parents not expecting a guest. Lee stayed there anyway, feeling unwelcome and fearing that he would be presented with a bill for room and board.[34]

Disliked by the boys, he tried to make up for it with the girls. From almost the beginning of his stay at Mount Hermon, he adored one Julia Winter, a student at Northfield Seminary, the nearby girls' school also founded by Dwight Moody. In his journals Lee wrote of her again and again, calling her "Jewel," hoping that she loved him, praying that she would be his wife.[35]

But he hardly spoke to her. In the presence of genteel white women, Lee bitterly regretted the social isolation of his Talladega childhood. At one party given by the Northfield girls, he spent the whole evening waiting in vain for Julia to speak to him—not realizing, he later said, that it was the gentleman's duty to begin the conversation. More than ignorance of etiquette was involved, however; his "courtship" was aborted by self-doubt. Bemoaning his "fate & face," Lee wished that he could "go right up & talk to any girl & not be bashful. Oh! if I were good looking!" During his two years at Mount Hermon, he never told Julia of his love and never got from her so much as a kiss. On graduation day he had the honor of delivering the Scientific Oration, but she did not bother to attend. When Lee visited her dormitory to bid a last good-bye, she came to the parlor and gave him a hearty handshake. After saying she had been glad to make his acquaintance, she hurried back to her room. "Was it to hide tears?" he wondered, "or to get to work packing, from which I had hindered her?"[36]

Although Lee did not learn much about women at Mount Hermon, his formal education continued. He studied Latin, physics, geometry, algebra, singing, and, of course, the Bible. His grades, judging by three extant report cards, ranged from "me-

dium" to "excellent-plus." As might be expected, his highest marks
were in physics, geometry, and algebra. He particularly enjoyed
working in the laboratory, and he won the respect and special
attention of his science instructor. Decades later the teacher recollected that "it was a daily delight to me to have you in my class,
for your mind ran so quickly and so far ahead of the lesson for the
day." Because of his outstanding record, Lee was elected to give
the Scientific Oration at his graduation. Besides excelling academ-
ically, he found time for worthwhile diversions. He joined the
Irving Literary Society, wrote poems, and attended lectures by
visitors like George Washington Cable and Russell Conwell (the
famous sermon "Acres of Diamonds" Lee found "very inspiring").[37]

On the whole, however, Lee disliked Mount Hermon, particularly the farmwork required of each boy. When he founded
the school, Dwight Moody had instituted physical labor as part of
the curriculum in order to build the students' health and character and to reduce the school's expenses by making it nearly self-
sufficient for provisions. Digging potatoes, however, had no attraction for Lee de Forest. Cursing "the diabolical system of making intelligent minds go to waste on senseless farm-work," he
swore that changes must occur before he would advise anyone but
a hayseed to come to "this punky little hole."[38]

One reason why he was there, however, was the low tuition
made possible by the work program: on his modest salary Henry
De Forest could not afford to send his son to a more prestigious
school. Lee recognized the need for economy. He had always tried
to be self-reliant; even back at Talladega he had earned money by
raising chickens, picking fruit, and (putting his scientific know-
how to use) electroplating silverware. While attending prep
school, he tried to relieve his father's financial burden by selling
books door-to-door during the summertime, a job he hated.[39]

But if Lee was willing to work hard to get money, he was even
more willing to spend it. Immediately after leaving home, he
squandered his small resources on soda pop and the like, prompt-
ing scoldings from his parents. At Mount Hermon he paid other
boys to do his chores and made a habit of borrowing cash from
friends.[40]

Financially pinched all through childhood and youth, Lee nur-
tured a dream of wealth. As early as 1891 he foresaw a time when
he would be "a very rich famous inventor." Certain that his scientific genius would make him a millionaire, he even planned how
he would spend his fortune. Someday, he vowed, he would repay

his parents for their years of hardship at Talladega. Someday he would honor his father by donating buildings to the college in his name. Someday.[41]

Despite their frequent quarrels, Lee had always acknowledged his father's virtues; after Lee left home, he could appreciate them even more. In March 1893 he wrote a respectful letter to "My Own Dear Father," congratulating him on his sixtieth birthday. De Forest could take satisfaction in the great and good things he had done, his son told him, and in the three children whom he had inspired to emulate his humanitarianism. "Although I am not called to be a minister or a teacher," Lee said, "I know that, if I am wise and diligent and good, the Lord will put in my way great opportunities for doing good."[42]

Henry De Forest, who brought schoolbooks and the Bible to the blacks of Alabama, had always encouraged good works. Combining the study of language with the inculcation of virtue, he had urged his children to adopt Latin mottoes by which to guide their lives. When Lee had settled on "to be a blessing," the Latin expression of which he later recalled, inaccurately, as *Esse Benedictus,* the father had been pleased. Now, years later, Lee still intended to follow his father's lead as a benefactor of mankind. Pledging to provide a huge endowment for Talladega, he confided that "some how, I feel and pray that the Lord will make me rich sometime, through my profession, and I will be of great use to humanity by my money." The conquistador came to the New World to serve God and get rich; Lee de Forest wanted to serve God *by getting* rich.[43]

Rich *and famous*—the second half of that fabulous cliché held an even greater attraction for Lee. All his life he strove for acclaim, and occasionally he succeeded. In May 1892 he got a long-desired and long-remembered taste of fleeting glory. At the semiannual Field Day exercises, he competed against two other boys in the mile walk and won. In a form "graceful and manly" (according to the school newspaper), he finished in eight minutes, twenty-six and one-quarter seconds, a new school record. The victory was hard-won. He had trained for weeks, measuring his progress with a stopwatch. Doubtless he savored the triumph because, as the newspaper reported, it came "contrary to the expectations of all." Half a century later, in his autobiography, he would recount the victory with glee.[44]

But he would not report the sequel. At the next Field Day, the following October, he lost the mile walk to a freshman who cut nine seconds off the record. Determined to beat the upstart, Lee swore that he would try again in the spring and "leave an enduring record for fame." In April, however, he found walking practice to be so "exhausting & scary" and time consuming that he decided not to enter the race. It was just as well, because in May the freshman champion broke his own record.[45]

Disappointed in sports, disgusted with farm labor, unsuccessful in friendship and love, Lee felt no regrets about leaving for college. He had escaped from the hostility of Talladega, only to find Mount Hermon no more hospitable. "Some of these Hermonites are the biggest babies & fools I ever saw," he wrote. "I hope I won't see any such down there at Yale." After two more years of hardship, better times were ahead. They had to be.[46]

2

I Wish to Excell: 1895

One day not long after his arrival at Yale, Lee was walking across campus when he was stopped by an upperclassman. "Let me look at you," demanded the older boy. "Why, you're the homeliest freshman I ever saw!" Three years later, at Lee's graduation, he was voted the homeliest member of the class. He had migrated from Talladega to Mount Hermon to New Haven, but he could not outrun his face. He himself thought his nose was too "rotund," his lips too thick, his features altogether too "niggerly." "I look so ugly," he confided to his diary, "that I sometimes feel content to commit suicide."[1]

Photographs of him during this period show a boy with big ears, bushy eyebrows, high cheekbones, thick lips, and a cranium peculiarly bulbous in back. Even his mother admitted that he had never been a handsome child. Yet, for all his physical imperfections, he was little uglier than the ordinary human being: plain rather than repulsive. It seems, then, that when his classmates named him "homeliest," they based their judgment on factors not strictly physical. Lee also was elected the "nerviest" man in the class; and while he received one vote as "brightest," he got sixteen for "thinks he is the brightest." Lee de Forest was not liked.[2]

At Yale he acquired a new nickname—"Tarheel," owing to his tendency to lapse into Southern colloquialisms—which seems not to have been a term of endearment. Although he spent much time in the company of other boys, he had no close friends. "How often," he recalled a month after his graduation, "have I felt a vague, half-recognized regret—a bitterness that I was thus alone—that others were not more cordial, better acquainted." After a university celebration with a crowd of noisy and rambunctious boys, he observed that "no other kind stays long with me—there is an estrangement—a lack of sympathy & respect."[3]

Nevertheless, Lee's Yale years were among his happiest. Although he lacked the company of the more thoughtful students, he at least shared the public amusements of the convivial. Unable

The college man, before and after. These photos from 1893 (above) and 1896 depict the student elected homeliest member of his class at Sheffield. Photos courtesy of Perham Foundation.

to find an intimate friend, he moved happily in a crowd. "Youth can offer no joy so full, so unique" as watching Yale win a football game—that was Lee's conviction. Ecstatic howls and hurrahs, hoarse singing and wild chants, hugging and screaming and leaping about after the Blue crossed the goal line—this constituted "the ideal event of a lifetime." Baseball games were no less sublime. After a game-tying home run with two out in the ninth, "I could *not* yell enough. I was impotent to ease my spirits, to express my bliss . . . I loved Yale as I never loved! Oh! what joy!! what joy!!!" (Yale won in the tenth.)[4]

Even off the ballfield, Yale provided plenty of delightful mob action. What could create more good fellowship than a freshman hazing, where Lee whacked the newcomers so hard that his arm grew numb? Or a campaign speech by William Jennings Bryan, where the Yalies hooted down the "graceless demagogue & agitator" from the West? Or an opera, where Lee amused his fellow music lovers by tossing a banana onto the stage? Yes, college provided many satisfactions. *"I love Yale,"* Lee announced. "This is the divine university."[5]

Indeed, he liked the place so much that he stayed there six years, three as an undergraduate (the standard term at Sheffield) and three more in pursuit of a Ph.D. Taking the mechanical engineering course at Sheffield, he enjoyed physics most but won a prize in chemistry. In 1895 he was unanimously elected to the editorial board of the *Yale Scientific Monthly*. In some areas of study, however, he did not do so well. He found German difficult and distasteful (his teacher considered him conceited) and Latin a waste of time. Meanwhile, Lee's drawing instructor pronounced him lazy.[6]

Not postponing his career until after he graduated, Lee worked on a number of inventions while in school. In 1894 he toiled over such devices as a "Double mirror illusion," an "Atmospheric Electric generator," and a "Photoscope" (whatever they were) and tried to imagine a way to convert light and heat into electricity (half a century later he would return to the problem of converting solar energy). In his first year as a graduate student he designed a machine for solving quadratic equations. One of the inventions that he found most exciting was the "airship." While working on the problem himself, he published an article in the *Yale Scientific Monthly* on "The Progress in Aerial Navigation." Writing eight years before the Wright brothers' success at Kitty Hawk, Lee predicted the "early attainment of aerial navigation by means of dynamic flying machines." He doubted that there was much future for balloons and dirigibles, but he foresaw an "enormous advance" in heavier-than-air machines. His foresight was impressive when contrasted to that of, say, the engineering editor of the *Times* of London, who as late as 1906 asserted that flying machines were "not only dangerous to human life but foredoomed to failure from an engineering point of view." Throughout his career, de Forest would scoff at experts' warnings that what he was trying to do was impossible.[7]

Lee was interested in both mechanical and electrical engineering, but gradually he concentrated on the latter. In March 1895 he was reading about Nikola Tesla (1856–1943), who had made important discoveries and inventions in the field of electricity. "His works," wrote Lee with admiration,

> are the greatest incitors to zealous work & study. How I *pray* that I may equal & excel him, that all the settled and forgranted beliefs in my genius & destiny are not idle visions of conceit. It would break my spirit to learn of it. I want *millions* of dollars.[8]

It would take a few years, however, to discover the research specialization that would allow him to make those millions. In December 1896 Lee thought that his "special first field of electrical enterprise" would be the development of the "condenser" (capacitor). Later he switched to the investigation of high-frequency electric oscillations, but in wires, not in free space. Radio historian Hugh Aitken points out that de Forest's Ph.D. dissertation, "Reflection of Hertzian Waves from the Ends of Parallel Wires," does not mention wireless communication. In later years de Forest would claim that when he was in graduate school he decided to make wireless his life's work. This claim may be true, but the documents from his graduate school years do not prove it.[9]

Plenty of documents do exist, however, which show how involved he was with a very different investigation, philosophy. He had been led into that tenebrous realm by his study of science. Drawing on evolutionism, empiricism, and materialism, he gradually assembled a new scheme of things to replace the Christian universe in which he had been raised.

December 10, 1893, was an important date in his life, for on that evening—a Sunday—he heard a professor of medicine lecture on the evolution of the human brain. The talk must have been exciting, because that night Lee wrote in his diary that he almost believed what the man had said. The following April Lee discovered that one could follow both Jesus and Darwin. After hearing the liberal Congregationalist preacher and editor Lyman Abbott speak on evolution and Christianity, he decided that "I am a half evolutionist." The other half did not hold out. After reading Darwinians Thomas Huxley and Herbert Spencer, Lee decided that the former's views coincided with his own, while the latter's work was "the broadest accomplishment *ever achieved* by the human intellect." By 1897 Lee wished that he could find a new "Church of Truth." "Their gospel shall be 'Universal Happiness,'" he declared, "and their scriptures 'Evolution.'"[10]

Preceding this conversion to evolutionary theory was a commitment to empirical method. In his Scientific Oration at Mount Hermon, Lee revolted against formalism ("artificial philosophy," as he called it). "The problems of the universe cannot be solved by thought alone," he announced. "True science began when man realized that discovery of physical truth consists not in its logical but [in its] experimental establishment." At Sheffield the next year he carried his empiricism even further. Disdaining metaphysics because it was "too theoretical" and contained "too much of the thingness of the wherefore," he said that the truths with which metaphysics dealt "must be discovered (if at all) through other channels than *mere* logic and reasoning—they must be got at by experiment and observed wherever such is possible." Thus, while noting that not every metaphysical problem could be solved, he maintained that the ones that *were* soluble would succumb to experiment and observation. At Mount Hermon Lee said that empiricism yielded physical truth; at Yale he said it revealed *meta*physical truth as well.[11]

This conflation of the physical and the metaphysical made sense to Lee because, while at Yale, he became a thoroughgoing materialist. On his twenty-first birthday he speculated that perhaps that which he had always called "God" was in fact "the finest, most supersensuous matter . . . This matter is eternal and infinite, perhaps is finer than the ether yet in coarser combinations & motions it exists in what we know as matter and wave motion." He ridiculed the idea of "spirit," saying that someday physical and psychological research would explain away that "vague, unsatisfactory chimera."[12]

Two years after reaching these conclusions, Lee received encouragement from Edgar Allan Poe. In the tale "Mesmeric Revelation," Poe's narrator (P) hypnotizes a dying man (V), then asks him questions about ultimate reality. Lee copied in his journal much of this dialogue:

P. Is not God immaterial?

V. There is no immateriality—it is a mere word. That which is not matter is not at all . . .

P. Is God, then, material?

V. No . . . He is not spirit, for he exists. Nor is he matter, *as you understand it.* But there are gradations of matter of which man knows nothing . . . These gradations of matter increase in rarity or fineness, until we arrive at a matter *unparticled*—without particles—indivisible—*one* . . . This matter is God. What men attempt to embody in the word 'thought,' is this matter in motion.

"Poe's conception of materialism & philosophy," Lee noted with satisfaction, "are very much like my own."[13]

A logician or metaphysician might have inquired why "unparticled matter" was not subject to the empirical test demanded of Christian doctrine, but such skepticism did not trouble the Sheffield undergraduate. To him it was clear that "Matter & motion are all." When he read Mary Baker Eddy's *Science and Health*—"the greatest libel on 'Science' I have yet seen"—he declared that the founder of Christian Science had everything backwards. All was one, as she said, "but I prefer to call this oneness Matter."[14]

When he began his metaphysical speculations, Lee thought he could reconcile old beliefs with new ones. "A knowledge of God," he said in his Mount Hermon Scientific Oration, "results from the right study of his creatures." Or, as he put it almost a year later, "the *open, unbiased* mind" could not offend the deity or harm the soul, "for God is truth." But as Lee's scientific studies led him to new sorts of truth, his idea of God was transformed rather than confirmed. By 1897 he rejected the notion of a personal God, "a mythical cruel monarch—a gigantic star-juggling *man.*" Doubting that scriptures were divinely inspired, Lee found mathematics a more reliable source of revelation. He trusted the mathematicians, he said, more than "the unshorn Isrealitish goatherds, crazed with Jewish mania."[15]

If science was a positive force pulling Lee away from Christian orthodoxy, life and death provided a negative force to repel him from the faith. As an empiricist, Lee had always demanded proof of God's existence and goodness. "I prayed for a fish," he reported in 1891, "& at once I got a bite." Unfortunately, the deity was not always so eager to show itself. In 1893 Lee entered a Bible-essay contest, prayed to win the fifty-dollar prize so that he could buy himself a bicycle, and felt certain that he would succeed—not

through his own efforts but through the kindly intervention of
Providence. When another boy won the prize, "my faith sustained
a blow."[16]

A much greater disappointment lay ahead. In January 1896 Lee
received a telegram from home saying that his father had suffered a stroke. "If God is the God *of love* as well as infinite
wisdom," Lee wrote in his journal, "he must interfere in nature's
processes in such cases. I *want* to believe He does. Can I, intel-
ligently?" The next day he got word that his father had died, and
he answered his own question in large, heavy, capital letters:
"NO." A few days later he made a new resolution for the conduct
of life. No longer would he rely on divine inspiration or destiny.
Henceforth, he would depend only on common sense, prudence,
and luck.[17]

After Henry De Forest died, his widow moved to New Haven,
where she began operating a boarding house. To economize, Lee
moved in with his mother, brother, and sister—an arrangement
that proved not altogether satisfactory. For some time Anna De
Forest had worried over her first son's "liberal tendencies"; now
that the family was reunited, religious conflict ensued. Lee tried
not to flaunt his apostasy: he continued to attend church services,
and he took his turn in saying grace at the supper table. "It seems
best to dissimulate and keep silent my views," he said, rather than
to hurt "the dear ones." But his mother could see where his heart
lay, and she bore in silence "a sorrow and an anguish."[18]

The lesson that Lee drew from all this was that people and
institutions must learn to change with the times. He pronounced a
curse on "Puritanism" for outliving its usefulness and wondered
whether people would ever realize that the old beliefs and prac-
tices must be discarded. As an evolutionist, Lee thought that
change was inevitable. As an inventor, he thought that change was
good. "God's great law," he said, "is *progress*."[19]

Whose law? Despite Lee's defection from Christianity, he never
doubted that there was some sort of God, a God whose true nature
had not yet been discovered. In 1896, when Lee thought that his
destiny lay in inventing an improved capacitor, he did not believe
that the capacitor was merely a useful and profitable electrical
device. "It is much more the stepping stone between the electrical
art of today & the finer, more etherial, mysterious, wavey form to
which we must come—it is a ladder to the finer realms of God."
When Lee said that God was "the finest, most supersensuous
matter," he was not denying God; he was deifying matter. Lee
found church services tedious, but when he contemplated physics,

he succumbed to religious awe. In 1925, when Manhattan was blacked out by its first total eclipse of the sun in 450 years, he felt

> a feeling of poignant regret, so deeply seated that it seemed to origi-
> nate in the very roots of ages—old heredity—unlike any mortal regret.
> Here for an instant we mortals lose all sense of self-consciousness—we
> become a thoughtless fragment of the infinite cosmos—the sun, the
> moon, the earth, of light, of electrons, of universal forces.

Lee was not merely being considerate when, in 1924, he told his mother that the difference between his religion and hers was a difference in "definition and expression" rather than in funda-mentals. "I firmly believe," he said, "in an Omnipotence infinitely above the mind of Man, and in the divinity of our evolution."[20]

As Lee's ideas changed, so did his behavior. When he first went North, he had heeded his father's admonition to "institute a quarantine against moral contagion." At summer camp in 1891 he was disgusted by cadets who smoked cigarettes and chased "chip-pies" (loose girls). At Mount Hermon he despised boys who told naughty stories. At Yale he resisted the urge to visit a theater "for men only"; and when invited to join in the traditional freshman drunk, he prayed, "From all such pernicious & degrading sur-roundings Deliver me, O Lord." Having taken the teetotaler's pledge, he could not accompany his chums when, after a football game, they marched from saloon to saloon.[21]

For some time Lee resisted temptation, but in the end Yale proved too much for him. On Christmas Day of his freshman year, he dined with his landlady, and she offered him a glass of hard cider. Not wanting to offend her, he took a sip, then swore never to drink again. In his senior year he attended a banquet where champagne was served. His "childish pledge" did not pre-vent him from partaking, but he promised afterwards never to drink *much* again. By June 1896 he was consuming enough beer to feel jolly, dance wildly, and make a spectacle of himself. And so it went with all Lee's resolutions. One spring day he bought a package of cigarettes: "I decided I could smoke one or two & not violate the spirit of my pledge." Six months later he bought a pipe. By the time he graduated from Sheffield, Lee was playing poker, shooting pool, and cursing.[22]

Lee's greatest temptation was sex, but his awkwardness with women delivered him from that particular evil. As soon as he arrived at New Haven, he was prowling the streets, following girls, catching hold of them, but getting left. One spring day a "chippie" smiled at him. He followed her, caught up, and strolled beside her. But when she asked him to buy her a drink, he walked away. "They don't pull my leg for a cent," he said.[23]

Lee was not always so tight-fisted. One evening he performed an expensive "experiment" suggested by one of his comrades. After inviting a young woman (whose nickname was Tom) up to his room, he treated her to refreshments. The beverages, however, failed to serve their purpose, for when Lee sought to cash in on his investment, "we nearly had a row." Although the experiment was a failure, the would-be Don Juan found that "my respect for Tom and womanhood was greatly increased." Five months later, on "a beautiful moonlight night—with songs and twinkling notes from a distant banjo, soft breezes—mellow light," Lee was at it again. Renting a rowboat (at twenty-five cents an hour), he took Tom for a ride on Lake Whitney. The lady, alas, proved as virtuous as ever, and "I didn't get my money's worth."[24]

Some women were cheaper than Tom. One named Inez proved "easy squeezing," and a waitress named Hattie was indiscreet. When Lee called on the latter, he had to be careful, lest her husband find out. Hattie and her spouse were separated, and Lee urged her to get a divorce. He wondered how a girl "so pure, so good, so sweet," could ever have married such a "brainless, shiftless, most repulsive gossoon." He considered it his mission "to preserve the flower unblighted" which that "mucker of a husband" had begun to wither. And if Lee could get in a few good squeezes while rescuing the damsel, so much the better. After an evening in his room with Hattie, during which "we smoked several cigarettes and were indiscrete," Lee recorded in his journal a new observation about the sexes. Although girls were ordinarily stronger than boys in resisting evil, he wrote, "the passion may be made so great that a boy can seduce her." Then, not wanting to give the reader of his diary the wrong impression, Lee quickly added a disclaimer: "but there was nothing of this done here."[25]

If not, it was just as well, for Hattie turned out to be not the kind of woman that Lee had thought she was—she went back to her husband. Now Lee saw the truth: Hattie was an "infinite fool, pitiful, *lustful* weakling" who "could not stand against her animal passions in face of her unspeakably better state when alone." Giving up his missionary work, he resolved not to try again to help one so unworthy of his confidence.[26]

During his Yale years Lee did not quite satisfy the cravings of the flesh. In large measure this continence was due to his ineptitude with women, but it may also be ascribed in part to a residue of conscience. The son of Henry De Forest could not easily forget that concupiscence was a sin. "I love to flirt," he wrote in 1893, "but am glad I never have any luck at it." Four years later, after he had dallied with a young nurse at the college infirmary named Lillian Laurence, he felt "hearty disgust and remorse." Again and again he vowed to quit "chippie-chasing"; again and again he felt "chagrin and contempt" when he broke his vow. Lee's misery was twofold. First he felt disappointed for not getting far with women. Then he felt ashamed for *trying*. In 1894 he recorded his mixed motives and unmixed woe:

> Am crazy after girls—lack strength, sense, manliness, don't improve all my opportunities, always resolve better but often repeat follies. Don't know my own opinions—lack the individuality of character my life's work demands—am a fool![27]

Frustrating as they were, Lee's sexual adventures were successful enough to cause him to explore a whole new world of ethics. As he drifted away from Christian theology, the young evangelist for science also cut loose from the old moral code. Pondering the "real law" regarding Hattie, he vowed that he would never act against his convictions but that he would try to get those convictions "*true* to *truth* if I can, whatever that may be." What was the new truth that would shape his convictions? Lee's researches provided an answer: evolutionism and what he called "utilitarianism" were "the right, God leading guides to our duties, our ideas, our ethics." Henry De Forest's version of religion, which inflexibly forbade one to covet the wife of one's neighbor, was a great inconvenience. Fortunately, evolutionism taught Lee that morality changes from time to time and that "Puritanism" was a creed outworn. Furthermore, Lee embraced "utilitarianism," maintaining that "the only criterion of right is this quality of an action for causing happiness, or preventing pain." As Lee interpreted utilitarianism, each individual had the prerogative of deciding whether a specific act would cause happiness or pain, and he welcomed that freedom. What Hattie's husband didn't know, wouldn't hurt him—and it might bring happiness to Hattie and Lee. So what was the harm of a little "indiscretion"?[28]

This line of reasoning was not entirely convincing, not even to Lee himself. In 1896 he went out with a woman and did "lots of squeezing." Afterwards he worried. "I must look out," he said, "or all my principles will be gone in this sweeping wave of rationalism

and philosophy that evolutionary belief has gradually developed
in me—I am not half as sure about the limit as I was when first I
embraced this belief."[29]

Lee de Forest used Darwinism to answer questions of personal
morality, but his ingenuity did not stop there. To him evolution
was "the all-solving and all-pervading key," the fundamental fact
of life. In this belief he was supported by Herbert Spencer, whose
ambitious work he found *inspiring,* wonderful." Scanning the
universe with an "unbiased eye" (as Lee saw it), Darwin's disciple
sifted out the "eternal principles" that were "discovered by trial,
warranted by *sense evidence.*" Starting with this empirically sound
base, Lee believed, Spencer rebuilt the whole house of knowledge:
"the inorganic and organic, biology, psychology, sociology, ethics—and all referred to fact." Thus a discovery in natural science
promised to revolutionize every aspect of thought and life.[30]

Evolutionary theory shaped Lee's thinking about the functioning of society. "God's great law is *progress, change,*" he declared.
"The world advances—it must advance." Defining a conservative
as *"an Adam who mistakes his epoch for the Mellenium,"* Lee always
considered himself a progressive. However, Lee's progressivism
did not entail any particular program, nor membership in an
organized movement. Instead, it was simply an enthusiasm for
reform, an eagerness to change society. Throughout his life he
applauded "those who do things, not discuss them eternally."[31]

Which things should be done? And for whom? Unlike some
progressives, Lee had little concern for what he called the "lower
class." In 1894 he wrote in his diary that "the Pullman & railway
strike at Chicago is awful & some one blunders and is cowardly or
mercifully unwise in not shooting down hundreds of the toughs &
foreigners who destroy property. Better for the country, to kill
them." In 1896 the twenty-three-year-old cast his first ballot—"for
McKinley & sound money, Nat'l honor, & higher civilization"—
and afterwards he noted with satisfaction that "the combined
forces of freak populists, selfish silverites, repudiators, anarchists,
rioters, jail birds, the lower strata of humanity—ignorant or vil-
lanous democrats—all the forces of wickedness combined—were
doomed by the other greater element that love honor and pros-
perity and law."[32]

Lee had not always been so hostile to the "lower strata of
humanity." Sometime around 1891 he had copied in his journal a
quotation from Oliver Goldsmith: "Law grinds the poor, And rich
men rule the law." Perhaps Lee's father, who taught school to
freedmen, had encouraged such sympathy for the poor. If so, the

influence did not endure. In 1893 Lee had to decide whether to help the poor or help himself, and he chose the latter. After taking a train to the Chicago world's fair, he found that he needed more money if he were to stay there long enough to examine all the marvelous machines on display. Fortunately for him, the men who pushed wheelchairs bearing disabled or weary or lazy tourists had gone on strike, and the company in charge of the grounds had advertised for strikebreakers. "Although it's against my principles to side against rather than *for* the poor men who push the chairs," he said, "I took a job as a chair-pusher yesterday because the idea of leaving the fairgrounds is like the idea of leaving heaven." By working overtime and by overcharging customers, Lee paid for a prolonged visit to the exposition. Thus, for the sake of science and self, he was willing to put political "principles" aside. Lee's abandonment of the poor was nicely recorded in his first journal. Reading over it in later years (as was his custom), he came across Goldsmith's statement that the law is an instrument of the rich. A reformed Lee de Forest now scribbled in a commentary: "Gold. was anarchist. Kill him."[33]

While paying no particular regard to the interests of the "lower class," Lee favored innovation in both foreign and domestic policy. After 1898, as Americans debated the wisdom of territorial expansion, Lee called stridently for a new frontier. When William Jennings Bryan denounced imperialism, Lee gave him a lecture on scientific politics. "To the Utilitarian mind," he wrote,

> trained in the great world truth of Evolution, nothing is plainer than that the course upon which our Nation is now entering is *inevitable.* Expansion is a world tendency . . . It is naught but the universal principle first found in biological evolution but none the less dominant in social development—the Survival of the Fittest . . . It is the destiny of a higher race to stretch out, to embrace and absorb the weaker; of an advanced civilization to supplant by force the inferior— of the Anglo-Saxon people to move west and south and dominate the Latin and Mongolian.

Bryan, who spent most of his life vowing to protect beleaguered farmers and laborers from the predations of Capital, would in his last years advocate a fundamentalist Christianity that valued all people, not just the "fittest." If the future "Defender of the Faith" read Lee de Forest's letter in 1898, he may have considered it just one more example of the pernicious effects of Darwin's theory.[34]

In his journal Lee amplified these ideas. Proud of his iconoclasm, he wanted the United States to divide China with England and Italy, somehow cutting out Russia, Germany, France, and Japan—a policy that he said was "radical and anti-traditional, and anti-spirit-of-our-forefathers, and unconstitutional, but withal, sensible and utilitarian." Mixing ethnic and economic motives, he hoped that "Anglo Saxon instead of Slav influences . . . shall decide the future trend of those teeming millions—the coming buyers of the world."

As an evolutionist, however, he did not believe that the Europeans could exploit China for long. Considering the Chinese a young and vigorous people, he predicted that as soon as they learned modern techniques of government and industrial production, they would throw off their masters. That would be disastrous for the English and the Italians, but not, fortunately, for the Americans, for the United States would still have "a whole *continent,* in a temperate zone—now occupied by decrepid and senile races of indians and Latins, to our individual monoply of developement." Lee predicted that eventually the "greater United States of America" would stretch from Alaska and Hudson's Bay to the Strait of Magellan. Looking still further ahead, he saw a time when even the greater United States would cease to be. It would be replaced by a World Republic and a Universal Race. Saxon, Slav, German, Mongolian—all would disappear into the global melting pot. Nevertheless, he assured himself, the "controling blend" in that amalgamation would be Anglo-Saxon.[35]

If Darwin served to justify foreign adventurism, he proved no less useful on the home front. American culture was evolving to ever higher stages, Lee believed. Although people of the present were still slaves to fashion, lust, money, liquor, and fatalism, someday they would be free. "Truly Evolution has done a good work," Lee said, "but she has just commenced, the race is young, we are far, very far, from the gods."[36]

How was this evolution to occur? Were people to wait patiently for the species to be perfected? Were they to wink at the liquor evil, for example, and at all the "terrors and disasters incumbent on all from its existence"? Should they endure the long evolutionary process of suffering and death required to make tipplers extinct? Naturally not. Having faith in man's ability to invent a better world, Lee wanted the government simply to forbid the sale of alcoholic beverages. Prohibition, he said, would "save our taxes one half, and the manufacture of idiots and insane almost completely; will promote universal morality and advance the world a century or more ahead of the time when the blind law of survival of the fittest has brought about the same."[37]

An interesting turnabout. When Lee discussed America's conquest of weaker nations, he argued that natural selection must be allowed to run its course. But when the enemy was alcohol, rational planning must supplant "blind law." Like other social theorists of the time, Lee found that Social Darwinism was a conveniently adaptable tool. Disagreeing for once with his mentor Spencer, who opposed government intervention, he advocated public supervision of tenements, sewers, and streets; wages-and-hours laws for women; and, good Republican that he was, a high tariff. He supported reformers like California Governor Hiram Johnson, and he worshipped Theodore Roosevelt.[38]

Lee de Forest's "progressivism" was of a piece with his faith in science and technology, because engineering, he believed, would improve the world. As an undergraduate, Lee foresaw the day when physical and social scientists would construct a heaven on earth. With "scientific research *the great* persuit & ultimate end," engineers would build rationally designed cities with rapid transit (airships) and cheap power. Technology would make physical labor unnecessary and would moderate the climate. Medical research would eradicate disease and perhaps even death. Hardly less startling would be the achievements of *social* engineers. Through research and planning, they would reverse recent history and make America a land of small cities, small farms, small businesses, and (despite all the regulations) small government. Through prohibition and universal education they would put an end to lust and to the consumption of alcohol and tobacco. No one would be allowed to produce more children than he could support—thus preventing overpopulation. Before long, fools would die out! "Let all help," said the visionary, "on progress of science: thus the millenium."[39]

Lee, then, was a "progressive," welcoming changes in life and thought, and expecting many of those changes to be induced by science and technology. His progressivism, however, was accompanied and partially nullified by an equally fervent Republicanism. While admiring Republican progressives like Hiram Johnson and Theodore Roosevelt, he despised the Democratic progressive Woodrow Wilson. Lee was happiest when he could support a man who represented both the GOP and reform; but if he had to choose between the two, he generally went Republican. Lee adored Teddy Roosevelt above all others, but he had no trouble endorsing William McKinley, Robert Taft, and Dwight Eisenhower, none of whom is ordinarily considered a champion of reform.[40]

Lee's support for political conservatives was made possible by his faith in science and engineering. Insofar as social improvement was produced by technology, politics was irrelevant. The *important* changes in society would be produced in research laboratories, not in the halls of government. This assumption was common during de Forest's heyday. Edward Bellamy and dozens of others who published utopian novels between 1883 and 1933 tended to equate progress with technological change. Lee de Forest, no less utopian and only slightly less novelistic, said in 1901 that the scientist, not the statesman, was "the pioneer, the most potent factor in civilization." Hence, even while voting for conservatives, the inventor could think of himself as a progressive. In summary, then, Lee's application of Darwinian theory to society *encouraged* him to favor political reform but did not *compel* him to do so. Although evolutionism inclined him to welcome social change, he could content himself—once Teddy Roosevelt was gone—with the changes wrought by technological advance. Airplanes and solar energy, not a New Freedom or New Deal, would usher in the millenium.[41]

Resolutely dedicating himself to engineering, Lee de Forest swore that life was "too short for novels." Nevertheless, he found time in college and graduate school for other sorts of literature. He relished Poe's "poetical style & new words" and "morbid grewsomeness"; called Ruskin a "Master of prose"; and found Ibsen's plays "splendid sermons." Unwilling to abandon a childhood dream, he wrote stories and poems himself. He submitted a tale to *The Youth's Companion,* but it was rejected. Sending a poem to *Chap Book,* he playfully enclosed a self-addressed postcard that bore this message: "If we admired your verses as much as we do your nerve in sending such a production to us, we would have inserted them on our front pages." The editors mailed him the postcard.[42]

All through his Yale years, but particularly after his father's death, Lee was strapped for cash. Busy as he was with his scientific, philosophical, and literary pursuits, he had to find time for making money. He tutored other students; worked for pay in the labs; waited on tables at restaurants; read meters for the gas company. Going for bigger money, he tried his hand as an entrepreneur. As a graduate student, he published and sold souvenir booklets for proms, turning a profit of from twenty-five to a hundred dollars in each of three years. Unfortunately, Lee also discovered that free enterprise has its pitfalls. He lost the bid for the right to produce the official souvenir book for an intercollegiate rowing regatta in June 1897. Undaunted, he decided to produce an unofficial one. Few people bought the unsanctioned book, and he lost hundreds of dollars. When Lee got home from the race, he found the sheriff waiting for him. After consulting a lawyer, the young promoter swore to pay off the debts he had incurred and was released from custody. In desperation he appealed to his acquaintances for loans, and with some success. His mother lent him a hundred eighty dollars; a professor, two hundred; one friend, twenty-five; another, fifty.[43]

Not everyone was so compliant. When he asked one hundred dollars of Lillian Laurence, whom he had been dating (and to whom he already owed twenty dollars), she dragged her feet. Lee was furious. "If her long lauded friendship can't get me that money," he vowed, "I'll tell her plainly I don't think much of it . . . Damn a friendship that can't cough up in a case of dire necessity like this!" Three months later Lillian still had not come through, and Lee decided that she was a "cowardly concealer and dissembler." Swearing that *his* affection would never have failed a "test of dollars," he told her that "we are no more to one another."[44]

In pursuit of lucre Lee was ingenious and persistent. He sent essays to literary contests and submitted puzzles and table games to Milton-Bradley. Trying to cash in on his mechanical talents, he tried to interest manufacturers in his designs: a compass, a micrometer, an ear cleaner, a pants creaser, a kerosene lamp, a bicycle with hydraulic gears, an underground trolley system—all to no avail.[45]

Aggravating Lee's penury was his improvidence. Ever since leaving home for prep school, he had lived beyond his means; and the coming years brought no improvement. As a graduate student, for instance, he found it necessary to buy a fancy bicycle, a golf suit, a new rug for his room, a boat ticket to New York to see a football game. After hearing a talk on "the problem of luxury," he felt momentarily conscience-stricken, but he quickly banished remorse, for "it does no good." Instead, he merely vowed, repeatedly, to mend his ways. "Just give me one more chance," he swore, "let me just get out of this financial hole & I shall be *so* saving, & *so* generous to Mama and Mary instead of to poor, miserable, selfish Me."[46]

After his father's death Lee felt pressure to leave graduate school and to find a job. Observing how hard his mother and sister worked to maintain the boarding house, he wished he could free them of that burden instead of adding to it through his own dependency. He noted also how his brother, who resented the drain on the family budget, called him a "parasite." Lee returned the hostility, considering Charles a hot-tempered lout and quarreling with him frequently.[47]

Lee was grateful to his sister and mother for their sacrifices, but his opinion of them was not unduly high. Mary, while "a good, kind, patient sister," was "narrow, dwarfed in many ways, and not pretty." For a "slow, pious man," he decided, she would make a choice wife. (As it happened, she eventually married a graduate of Yale Divinity School.) Like daughter, like mother. Lee loved his mother and later recalled fondly her saintly influence. But in 1897 he bridled at her piety and moralism, longing to be "where one was not afraid to say d--n if he so pleased." Later that year he got his wish. He left the boarding house and moved into Yale's West Divinity Hall.[48]

As for "romance," Lee was no more successful at Yale than at Mount Hermon. The new object of his adoration was Helen Wyatt of Medford, Massachusetts, his own second cousin. Kin, however, proved less than kind. After pleading with Helen for a year, Lee finally persuaded her to go with him to the junior prom in January 1897. Eagerly anticipating the event, he wondered whether *this* relationship might develop into love; and to help it along, he took dancing lessons. But the weekend brought no delight. Lee found his date "cross and hard to please." At the prom she gave him only two dances, making him feel "grieved and ferocious." He observed that she seemed to have a slight cold, but he thought little of it.[49]

Two days later, when her malady was diagnosed as appendicitis, Lee was more willing to forgive her for neglecting him at the prom. "Despite the $20 already spent on her," he bought her thirteen white roses and he saw "more and more in her to admire, beneath all this petulant & girlish vanity." Two weeks later, however, when he visited her at the hospital, she frankly offered insults to himself and, what was worse, to Yale. The devotee of the divine university had to swallow his anger. On March 2 he visited her again, resolved to tell her off at last. When he informed her of the chance she had lost by killing his growing love for her, she said that the idea was absurd and that something in her had always rebelled at the sight of him. "I wonder if it is so," he wrote in his journal with his usual optimism, "or her childish fancy of the moment." A year later he found himself falling more and more in love with Helen.[50]

Knowing that he was not handsome, Lee sought to develop other charms. "Truly if I would ever demand, deserve, or recieve the *love of women & especial* respect of men," he wrote in 1895, "I must be brilliant, win fame, show the greatness of genius & to no small degree." Antagonized by his family, despised by his schoolmates, rejected by women, Lee had always felt compelled to fight for esteem. To force the world to respect him, he used his mind as a weapon. His scientific study was motivated at least as much by personal ambition as by intellectual curiosity. Noting in 1895 that discoveries would earn him "credit" in men's eyes, he wrote in his diary that "I wish to excell."[51]

During that same year, his class at Sheffield formed a chapter of Sigma Xi, the scientific honorary society, and Lee resolved to be a member. Passed over in the first election, he anxiously awaited the next. But when, "to my chagrin & surprise," he was left out again, he was furious. Claiming that "almost every pimp & jerk in all Sheff's notorious crew of half-shot instructors" was a member of the society, he explained to himself that those "bum instructors" had blackballed all the "highstand men, & original men." In his journal he recorded a vow: "I shall show them someday what a mistake they made. I will honor *them* & not they *me!*"[52]

Lee de Forest had no low opinion of his ability and potential. Not long after first failing election to Sigma Xi, he said "candidly, without conceit, I am a *long, long* way in advance of my times." Half a year later when his hard-pressed family urged him to forgo further graduate study, he refused to listen, "for my *whole destiny* depends on it." His continuing in school, he decided, was "all important for the further future, for life, for destiny, & for the world."[53]

To sustain this immense self-confidence, Lee took heavy doses of Emerson. On his desk calendar he scribbled "stimulants to my progress," one of which was a quotation from "Self-Reliance," and he read that essay again and again. Sometimes, though, he almost doubted. In March 1895 he observed apprehensively that it would break his spirit to learn that his faith in his genius was misplaced. The following year he said that such a discovery would be worse than death.[54]

Lee felt destined for greatness, but, paradoxically, he feared that his "destiny" might elude him. With so much at stake, he took no chances. In 1893 he even passed up an opportunity to become a Horatio Alger hero. "I had a chance to stop a runaway horse," he reported, "but as visions of my future usefullness blasted by a reckless death, flashed accross me I gave it up & went to the Reading room & read Puck instead." Although acknowledging that the war with Spain in 1898 was "a *holy struggle* for humanity, and liberty, and truth," Lee found that his true duty was to stay in graduate school. If he were to join the army, "my life would be thwarted & turned aside, probably I would miss my destiny."[55]

After a brief delay, however, Lee volunteered. Confident that the war would not last more than six months, he calculated (correctly) that by the time he could be inducted, trained, and shipped south, Cuba would already be taken. "I will get the benefits—*and the glory (!)* of the campaign," he wrote, "without the danger. I do not risk my destiny—I think." Glory without danger was a strong attraction, but Lee also had other reasons for joining up. Feeling that he had lost interest in "the realities of life," the graduate student felt that military training would build him up physically and make him "very much more of a man." Moreover, Lee intended to join the "Yale Battery," and he looked forward to the camaraderie of camp and field with his fellow volunteers from New Haven. "I have had too little—far too little Yale fellowship in my undergraduate life," he noted. "Here, after it is long past—is another chance."[56]

And another disappointment. Enlisting too late to get into the college contingent, Lee found himself in a regular outfit with "a pretty nasty lot of farmers." After a "shallow, unsatisfying" summer in camp at Niantic, Connecticut, he was mustered out and returned to Yale.[57]

Unwilling to let his destiny be jeopardized by runaway carriages or splendid little wars, Lee de Forest would not tolerate less deadly inconveniences. When he needed a peg board on which to string out a wire, he simply pounded nails into the oak table in a lab. When advised to lay down his tools during a lecture, he continued working until he blew a fuse and plunged the lecture hall into darkness. "I am prone to be very reckless, in all things—as Father so often told me," he confessed, "—loaded with gaul & nerve— thoughtless of other's rights." This troubled him, but only because it might cost him a job.[58]

When Lee blew out the lights in Winchester Hall, he discountenanced "chump Hastings"—Professor Charles Hastings—an enemy of long standing. As an undergraduate, Lee had gone to Hastings with the idea for an invention, a device that would send the exhaust steam from an engine (instead of the usual cold water) back into the boiler, thus saving energy. Hastings had declared the idea impracticable and thereby had earned Lee's everlasting enmity and contempt. He was not the only professor with that distinction. In 1895, when Lee's article on aerial navigation failed to win a contest, Lee said it was because his subject was too novel for "old fogy Professor Dubois," the contest judge. Convinced that he was a long, long way in advance of his time, Lee despised those pedestrian minds that could not recognize his genius.[59]

In 1891, before leaving Talladega, Lee remarked that *Daniel* was his favorite book of the Bible, but he did not say why. Perhaps, while fending off stones thrown by neighbors and resisting his father's arguments against science as a vocation, he imagined himself keeping the faith as he walked through a fiery furnace. Perhaps he saw himself surrounded by false wise men who could not read the writing on the wall. Or perhaps he looked forward to the day when he would emerge from the lion's den and cast all his enemies into the pit. At summer camp in 1891 he drew a gruesome sketch in his notebook: a ring-nosed savage holding a dripping sword in one hand and a severed head in the other. At Yale in 1893, after the last run-in with Professor Hastings, Lee swore that "someday revenge will come."[60]

3

The Driven Ones: 1904

In August 1899 Dr. Lee de Forest moved to Chicago to take up his first full-time, permanent job: a position in the dynamo department of the Western Electric Co., the manufacturing arm of American Telephone & Telegraph. It was not all that he had hoped for. The pay was low (eight dollars a week), the day long (ten and a quarter hours), and the work uninteresting (to someone who recently had acquired a passion for wireless telegraphy). Even after he was transferred to the company's telephone laboratory, he was restless. After dull days conducting experiments on telephone cables, he spent his evenings at the library excitedly reading about the latest developments in wireless.[1]

After a month at Western Electric, de Forest wrote to Guglielmo Marconi, then to Nikola Tesla, asking to be made an assistant. "It has been my greatest ambition since first working with electric waves," he told Marconi, "to make a *life work* of that study." He did not get a job with either of the famous inventors, but in the spring of 1900 he got his chance with the American Wireless Telegraph Co. of Milwaukee. "At last, *at last*," he exulted in his journal, "after long planning & plotting & years of study & weeks of patient weary waiting, I have the opportunity offered for the work I have chosen—Experimental work in *wireless telegraphy*—on the Lake first—then with the navy, then *navies*, foreign travel, scientific investigation—success!"[2]

But the dream was not easily realized. While with Western Electric, de Forest had used company time and equipment to develop what he called the "Responder," an electrolytic detector of wireless signals. With American Wireless he continued to work on it, again at company expense. But when the firm's president sought to make use of his employee's invention, de Forest refused. "I will not let it go into the hands of any company," he said, "until that company is mine." The brash inventor was fired.[3]

Returning to what he called "Skunk City" (Chicago) in September 1900, de Forest resorted to part-time jobs: assistant editor of

the *Western Electrician,* then lecturer at the Lewis Institute. In
return for minor services, he was allowed by Professor Clarence
Freeman to use the electrical laboratories at the Armour Institute.
He also conducted experiments in the rented rooms in which he
lived. In such privacy and with such freedom, de Forest enjoyed
his work, "for it is all my own & for myself . . . It would be hard
for me to drop it & go back to a task in a great shop, or under any
employer."[4]

From an economic standpoint, however, he was not entirely
self-reliant. His roommate, Edwin H. Smythe, an engineer for
Western Electric, lent him five dollars a week, which enabled him
to keep working on a wireless system and entitled Smythe to a
share of whatever revenues that system might produce. It was
Smythe who paid the fees for de Forest's first patent application
and was co-holder of the patent. De Forest also entered into
partnership with Professor Freeman, whose wireless experiments
were already well known in Chicago. Both Freeman and Smythe
collaborated with de Forest in research.[5]

In July 1901, de Forest and his associates made the first long-
distance test of their wireless system, successfully transmitting
from the Armour Institute to the Lakota Hotel, a mile away.
Shortly thereafter they installed a transmitter on a yacht belonging to a friend of Freeman and, sailing out on Lake Michigan, sent
dots and dashes that were received on the mainland. This last
event was covered in newspapers. "It was my first taste of publicity," de Forest later recalled. "I liked it."[6]

But he was not satisfied. Devoting most of his time to work on
wireless, he resented the fact that it was only a sideline to his
collaborators. "Smythe's aid was & has been small enough," he
grumbled. "I have wagered all." What was more, he resented
having to share the credit for any accomplishments. Indeed, de
Forest found himself obscured in the shadow of Freeman, who
had already achieved a following among the Chicago press corps.
Therefore, in the summer of 1901, de Forest sought to escape
"Freeman's fame" and "the impossible attitude of Freeman &
Smythe" by transferring operations from Chicago to the vicinity
of New York City.[7]

The partners objected. They warned that capital would be hard
to obtain in New York, and they may not have wanted de Forest to
be far away from them and beyond their control. But he insisted.
In late August he moved the laboratory to Jersey City and crowed
over his "diplomatic triumph." Noting in his journal that having
"two Chicagoans, in Chicago, desiring to operate from there" was

intolerable, he observed that "*my fame*, my independence of management, my whole future possibilities required the start to be made here."[8]

De Forest's first big project on the East Coast was to provide wireless reportage of the 1901 America's Cup yacht races. Two years earlier Marconi had covered the regatta for the New York *Herald,* and the wireless reportage itself had become a front-page story. "MARCONI WILL REPORT THE YACHT RACES," hollered the headline in the *Herald* for 1 October 1899. "COMPLETE DETAILS OF THE MARVELLOUS INVENTION BY WHICH NEWS IS REPORTED FORTY MILES AWAY WITHOUT THE USE OF WIRES." After receiving such publicity in 1899, Marconi's associates planned to cover the 1901 America's Cup races for the Associated Press. This time, however, they would face a challenger, for Lee de Forest had signed a contract with the AP's rival, the Publishers Press Association.[9]

Time was short. Although President McKinley's assassination postponed the races for several weeks, de Forest's team had to work day and night in order to install a transmitter on a tugboat and a receiver on land (near Sandy Hook, New Jersey). Dissension among the de Forest group did not help. Freeman, who bankrolled much of the venture, insisted that they use a new transmitter he had invented; but de Forest, after trying it, dumped it overboard and installed another.

The struggle against time, untrustworthy hardware, and unhelpful partners robbed de Forest of his usual vigor. A week before the races he suffered a physical breakdown and was sent to the hospital. After three days' rest he returned to work—"rose before dawn, tottered to the boat, worked feverishly"—and on the day of the regatta he was ready. The boats got under way; de Forest's telegrapher tapped away on the tugboat while Marconi's sent dots and dashes from a nearby yacht; and on shore . . . no signal was heard. In those early days of wireless, no one had mastered the art of tuning. As a result, the Marconi and de Forest teams succeeded only in jamming each other's signals. When they realized what they were doing, they agreed to take turns transmitting; but that arrangement worked only briefly. Soon a third wireless operator began transmitting, thus causing interference that prevented reporting of the races. Despite claims to the contrary, no wireless telegrapher successfully covered the yacht races of 1901.[10]

After losing at the races, de Forest was even more disgusted with his colleagues. He found that, as they had warned him, it was difficult to raise capital in New York; but rather than acknowledge that they had been right, he complained that they did not help him enough. As he trooped from financier to financier, he noted resentfully that his collaborators, "the Chicago leeches," collected "fat salaries" while doing little.[11]

De Forest also was not impressed by the foresight of businessmen. Finding few who thought wireless telegraphy a profitable investment, he bemoaned the "microscopic mentalities" of the giants of industry. Frustrated by the caution of his partners and patrons, the audacious inventor—again a long, long way ahead of his time—looked forward to the day when he would be "freed from the shackles & impediments of my fool friends."[12]

After several false starts de Forest in January 1902 arranged the incorporation of the American De Forest Wireless Telegraph Co. Not having kept Freeman and Smythe fully informed of his plans, he surprised them by naming the company after himself. In March the Chicagoans stormed back east, "rankling mad," and insisted that either *De Forest* be dropped from the firm's name or *Smythe* and *Freeman* be added. De Forest would not allow it. "From the start," he said, "I have had the one aim in view, to make my name at least rank with that of Marconi, and to now allow these men . . . to further climb into prominence by the ladder of *my* ability & *my* bitter sacrifice & effort—would have been more than I could further endure."[13]

To promote and direct the company, de Forest had obtained the services of a remarkable entrepreneur. Originally named Abraham Schwartz, this canny and creative Texan had changed his name to Abraham *White* to brighten his image as a businessman. Described by *Success Magazine* as a "Colonel Sellers in flesh and blood" (a reference to a slippery character in Mark Twain and Charles Dudley Warner's *The Gilded Age*), he had made his fortune by investing in real estate, inventing fireproof chemicals, and speculating in government bonds. Bold and resourceful, he seemed the perfect president for a wireless company.[14]

White built up American De Forest by selling stock. These sales raised capital that enabled the company to sell wireless apparatus at a very low price, thus excluding competitors. To sell stock, however, White had to use ingenuity—which, indeed, he had in abundance. He issued false press releases, announcing that American De Forest had absorbed the American Marconi Co. and had had its system adopted as the official system of the U.S. Navy and Signal Corps. The company's advertising brochures claimed that if someone invested a few hundred dollars in the company now, he would thereby guarantee financial independence for his children. Eventually, however, investors found that their money was not put to the purposes they had intended. For example, American De Forest sold fifty thousand dollars of stock for a station in Atlanta, spent three thousand building the station, and never used it to transmit a dot or a dash.[15]

Observing this fiscal legerdemain, de Forest had some qualms but managed to suppress them. In July 1902 he said that Abraham White "has been to me all & more than a Brother." Although he would sometimes question White's "bias towards the stock selling" and his "indifference to many just and imperative obligations," he admired his "courage, enthusiasm, grit, and generally his loyalty to me." As late as July 1904 he considered White "that Prince among Men" and "the friend of a hundred life-times."[16]

The company's first years were busy ones and not without

The man in the pin-striped suit, 1905. With bowler hat shading his eyes, cigar jutting from mustachioed lip, watch fob cavalierly exposed, and dutiful assistant Charley Cooper attending at his side, de Forest radiates the early success of the American De Forest Wireless Telegraph Co. Photo courtesy of Perham Foundation.

success. In 1902 American De Forest reported war maneuvers for the Signal Corps and sold its first wireless sets to the navy. The following year de Forest, who served the company as vice president, director, and chief engineer, demonstrated the "American system" to the British, who, however, weren't buying. The trip to England proved useful, though, for on the return voyage in January 1904 De Forest met London *Times* correspondent Lionel James, who was on his way to the Orient, where Russia and Japan were edging toward war. Excited by the journalistic possibilities of wireless, James arranged to have a de Forest transmitter installed on a dispatch boat in the Pacific; and when the first gun fired on Port Arthur, James and his boat were there. Until the Russians forced him to cease sending bulletins, wireless telegraphy enabled him to scoop his rival reporters by hours or even days.[17]

On land, too, the American De Forest Wireless Telegraph Co. scored successes. In 1904 the company erected a station at the World's Exposition in St. Louis, and from there it sent messages as far as Chicago. Because the company received remuneration for many of the wireless telegrams, de Forest announced happily that "the day of *Revenue* has at last arrived." And thanks to an unusually low level of static interference that summer, the transmission was good enough to win for the company an Exposition Grand Prize and Gold Medal. In that same year the Navy contracted with the firm to build powerful stations in Puerto Rico, Florida, Cuba, and Panama. "A bright day," de Forest rejoiced, "has at last broken." As chief engineer, he personally supervised construction at the sites.[18]

On 5 April 1903, as he neared his thirtieth birthday, de Forest took stock of his condition: "Self-satisfaction—boundless ambition—but no romance." In his first half dozen years after leaving Yale, his love life did not keep pace with his rising scientific career.[19]

Having lost interest in Helen Wyatt, de Forest turned to an acquaintance from childhood, Jessica Wallace of Council Bluffs. During the summer after finishing graduate school, he stayed with the Wallaces (friends of his father) for a full month, reading poetry to Jessica and taking her for boat rides on a lake. By the time he left for Chicago, he felt that her affection was secure. But in September she wrote to tell him that she could not love him—a statement that he found incomprehensible. Borrowing ten dollars, he took a train to Iowa and tried to win her. She remained firm, but he vowed that *"she will turn."* In January 1900 he reproached her for jilting him; and, as with Helen Wyatt, he saw an affront to himself as an affront to his beloved alma mater. "Is this your thought of the true & constant," he asked, "and is it *thus* you interpret *Yale?*" Apparently he had given Jessica a timepiece that hung on a necklace, for he warned her that if she did not come back to him, "each tick of the little watch above your heart (if you can wear it) will become a throb of pain because it means 'true', 'faithful', 'loyal', 'Blue'." Two and a half years later de Forest ended a letter to "My dear Comrade" with the pledge "Semper fidelis."[20]

This is not to say that he pined away for the rest of his life in hopeless adoration. In April 1903 he visited the Wallaces again but found that doom had visited first. Jessica's brother had committed suicide; her despondent father seemed to be losing his mind; her sister was sickly, nearly an invalid. Jessica herself "has been falling away for a year, a shadow now—the seeds of death within her frame." Such misfortune thrilled the imagination of an admirer of Poe. "The *Fall of the House of Wallace* is at hand," he wrote. "Thank God that I am not of it—that a harsh, but kindly fate, saved me from my early self & for my greater destiny!"[21]

During these early New York years de Forest "played the dog." He took strolls through Battery Park with one "Nanet" and wrote a poem to a barmaid named Kathleen. With a woman whose name he did not record, he sailed down the Hudson in the moonlit cabin of a ferry. With at least two of his girlfriends de Forest thought of marriage. In December 1904 he was being congratulated on his engagement to one Marie, but apparently the couple were soon disengaged, because in April 1905 he was pleading with Jane McEnery, daughter of U.S. Senator Samuel D. McEnery of Louisiana, to elope with him—despite the fact that she was scheduled to marry another man in two weeks. Such an elopement appealed to de Forest, offering "all those elements of romantic suddenness, departure from the well-beaten ruts of society marriage, and certainty for universal notoreity which I have long desired." But Miss McEnery refused.[22]

In truth, de Forest was not certain he wanted a wife. As his desire for "notoreity" suggests, he had other priorities. In December 1905 he observed that his "fine lover's frenzy" never lasted long, that his work in wireless always made him lose interest in women. Moreover, he could not find a woman who lived up his ideal, what he called the "Golden Girl." To satisfy him a spouse would have to be a musician and an artist, "to call back to a weary heart the long-lost years when I trod thru fancies' Fairy land." She

must be tender and sympathetic to his moods. While decidedly
spiritual, she could not be "narrowly religious," for de Forest was a
free thinker who roamed with Emerson and Huxley. If she were
all that and loved him, he decided, he would be happy at last.[23]

As it turned out, however, he settled for a little bit less. On 17
February 1906, he married Lucile Sheardown, an employee in a
publishing house. Since his journals and letters do not mention
her between their meeting in October 1905 and their separating
in March 1906, it is difficult to say what he originally saw in her.
There is no problem, however, in discovering his later opinion.
Immediately after the wedding the couple sailed for England, but
it was not much of a honeymoon. During the voyage and in the
weeks that followed, Lucile would not allow him to consummate
the marriage, brusquely repulsing his advances. Understandably,
this behavior "baffled & maddened me." Moreover, he recalled,
she constantly complained of flaws in his character and behavior,
publicly ridiculing him at every opportunity.[24]

De Forest knew he was not perfect. "I admit my selfishness," he
said, "that my work, my success in life has made me to some extent
imperious, over bearing, impatient; yet (I swear it) I have done all
things in my power, as I could see the way, to make Lucile happy."
He believed he had given her everything: wealth, social position,
affection, consideration, opportunity for travel and study, and a
gifted companion for life. And what had she given him? "Never a
word of hearty thanks."[25]

Quickly he discovered that she was no Golden Girl. She de-
tested poetry and, while in England, never once felt "the charm of
historic associations." Instead she gave herself over to shopping,
eating, and sleeping. After five months of what passed for marriage, de Forest observed that his bride was surly, indifferent, and
misanthropic. Gradually he put together a theory to explain her
unnatural behavior. She was, he decided, the mistress of a rich
man and had married himself only to acquire respectability. "After
all these years," he moaned, "I find a harlot where I sought a
wife." Two months later, when suing for divorce, he claimed that
his bride had had an affair with the president of a brewing
company.[26]

These were days of misery. "My life since I married," wrote the
young engineer, "has been largely framed in cycles, my days &
moods & emotions bounded by a periodic curve—and usually of
negative sign—below the abscissa of happiness or content." Less
than a month after the wedding, de Forest and Lucile resolved to
separate. Later attempts at reconciliation always failing, the unlov-

ing couple were divorced after long litigation in December
1907.[27]

If de Forest's marital troubles kept him below the abscissa of
happiness, professional setbacks plunged him clear off the chart.
As early as August 1905 he had begun to quarrel with Abraham
White, "the friend of a hundred lifetimes" and the president of
American De Forest. White, always an adventurer, had committed
the company to headlong expansion, rapidly erecting wireless
stations across the continent. De Forest, as chief engineer, advised
against that policy, saying that static interference made overland
transmission uncertain. He argued that the company should play
it safe by concentrating on marine wireless, even though that less-
spectacular policy might attract fewer investors. White's expan-
sionism prevailed, however, and the company ended up with an
array of expensive and inefficient inland stations.[28]

Sometimes, however, de Forest's expertise *was* respected, but
with consequences almost as bad. The company's wireless system
used an electrolytic detector that was an improved version of the
"Responder" de Forest had developed in Chicago. Although his
method of improving the device had been to copy a detector used
by rival inventor Reginald Fessenden, de Forest assured his employers they were free to use the Responder, without fear of
infringing on a Fessenden patent. In 1906 a federal court
disagreed, issuing an injunction against American De Forest. The
company's officers were not pleased with their scientific adviser.[29]

How displeased they were is an open question. De Forest's
sometime associate Lloyd Espenschied recalled years after the fact
that the directors were so incensed by their chief engineer's erroneous counsel that they fired him. De Forest's autobiography
acknowledges that they doubted his competence, but his journal
entries indicate that he left the company by choice. In 1906
American De Forest was deep in debt. In a salvage operation,
White created a new company, the United Wireless Telegraph Co.,
transferring American De Forest's assets to United and leaving its
debts in the hulk of the old firm. De Forest was disgusted with
White, apparently for both practical and ethical reasons. He lamented that a promising industrial proposition had been miscon-
ceived, mismanaged, and deserted, and he wished that it had been
entrusted to a man of conservative business sense rather than to a
showman. In November 1906 he resigned from American De
Forest and swore to try to prevent further prostitution of his
name in "this wretched stock swindle." Cashing in his twenty

percent of the stock, he received in return five hundred dollars plus the rights to pending patents held by the company.[30]

The inventor was heartbroken by the demise of his namesake, American De Forest. "This," he exclaimed after his resignation, "is the funeral of my first-born child!" With both his company and his marriage defunct, he had nothing to leave to posterity. *"But my work goes on,"* he vowed; then grimly added, "while I live."[31]

From 1899 to 1906, as during most of his life, de Forest's income fell short of his need. In Chicago he lived in a small, cold room; during his early days in New York his overcoat grew threadbare. But in spite of forced economizing, his tastes remained expensive. When he got a raise of two dollars a week from Western Electric, he planned to move into a steam-heated flat, to have his shoes shined twice a week henceforth, and to buy a phonograph and an automobile; after launching American De Forest, he invested in sporty suits and bowler hats. Wherever he went—New Haven, Chicago, Milwaukee, New York—he borrowed money from relatives and friends. Indeed, one cause of his break with Abraham White was the latter's refusal to give him additional personal loans. White's friendship, like Lillian Laurence's, had failed the test of dollars.[32]

Constantly in debt, disappointed in love and business, de Forest needed a reason to go on. Late in life he was to recall that memories of persevering ancestors had inspired him to endure those years when every dream exploded. Maybe so. But his journals and letters of the period record no such motive. Instead they reveal sources of strength that were less familial than individual. In 1902 he explained to Jessica Wallace why he devoted his life to research:

> Down there in the dim light, often at night, among batteries and coils of wire & chemicals, I know there are many strange things awaiting— laws of which I have dreamed, but yet know vaguely only—There lurks unseen the material of strange structures, miracles of Science, Castles of fame—and often in quiet hours, when for an Instant I realize in part the nobility of the great unknown, I half-believe I hear faint voices calling to me—Whispering some great secret!

Faint voices calling him to castles of fame—Lee de Forest never lost faith in his destiny. In the year he wrote this letter, before he had made any major inventions, he was sufficiently certain of his future greatness to begin writing his autobiography.[33]

The promise of future glory, however, was not his sole motive for studying electricity. As his letter to Jessica indicates, he was thrilled by physical reality itself—strange structures, miracles of science. In 1891 he copied in his journal Newton's statement that he felt "like a boy playing on the sea shore and diverting my self in now and then finding a smoother pebble, or a prettier shell than ordinary, whilst the great ocean of truth lay all undiscovered before me." Two years later, in his Mount Hermon Scientific Oration, de Forest described several recent discoveries, then exclaimed, "If these are but pebbles picked up from the shore of the great ocean of truth, what are the mysteries hidden in the mighty unexplored!" At Yale a few years later, as he studied energy and light, he found himself inspired to "enter into that tenuous realm that is the connecting link between God and mind and lower matter." When he spoke of science and of his career in it, he sounded like a prophet—or a Faust:

> I shall soar higher and plunge deeper—shall peer further, than they all. I shall learn to weigh an atom, and circumscribe a vortex ring— shall guess its shape and invent the few primeveal knots and intertwinings that make up the several elements . . . I shall plan how the gold and silver may be interchanged, and invent a reason [for] the universal cause of energy and prophesy the last and final destination. *Gravitation—Electricity,—Thought,—Life,—God*—these notions must be analysised.

For Lee de Forest, science was a religious quest.[34]

But if personal fame and religious knowledge were two alluring objectives, the progress of humankind was a third. In the late nineteenth century American agnostics pledged, in the words of the notorious iconoclast Robert Ingersoll, "to render all the service possible in the holy cause of human progress." Practicing (or at least preaching) a religion of humanity, agnostics found justification for existence in improving the lives of their fellows. In the 1860s the young scientist William James worked himself out of despondency over the disappearance of God by considering his opportunity to "add to the welfare of the race":

> And if we have to give up all hope of seeing into the purposes of God, or to give up theoretically the idea of final causes, and of God anyhow as vain and leading to nothing for us, we can, by our will, make the enjoyment of our brothers stand us in stead of a final cause; and through a knowledge of the fact that that enjoyment on the whole depends on what individuals accomplish, lead a life so active, and so sustained by a clean conscience as not to need to fret too much.

Like Henry Wadsworth Longfellow chanting his "Psalm of Life," William James advised people to escape fretful depression by hurling themselves into action. It should not, however, be just any kind of action but that which would contribute to "the mass of work which each generation subtracts from the task of the next." There were many different ways to help posterity:

> You may delight its senses or "taste" by some production of luxury or art, comfort it by discovering some moral truth, relieve its pain by concocting a new patent medicine, save its labor by a bit of machinery . . .

William James saw plenty of important work for the inventor.[35]

Lee de Forest, too, saw his chance. Indeed, he thought that the inventor had an advantage over every other kind of "genius." In 1898 he said that the artist or musician's work is "transient" because it produces no "real uplift to mankind," but the scientist's work has more "effects *in good.*" Still trying "to be a blessing" (following his childhood motto), he said in 1901 that "the scientist who can learn of Nature's secret and lessens the fierceness of human life, has the highest of callings." In 1904 he wrote a poem that began in egotism and ended in philanthropy:

> We are the Driven Ones
> Forced forever forward by the aims
> A rash ambition which was born in us
> Has conceived and borne to scourge.
>
> .   .   .
>
> And this our one reward (so be our aims are noble)
> That our race is better for our lives as slaves,
> O pity us, the Driven Ones![36]

De Forest's mother took pity on him. Fearing that he would break down under the intense and constant pressure of his vocation, she prayed every morning and every night that God would reveal himself to de Forest as "your Father & your Friend," and she begged her son "not to think you are equal to your need, but to look to Him for leading." Meanwhile, the inventor called himself "an old agnostic" and worked far into the night, even on Sundays and holidays, in search of "the great unknown."[37]

4

At Last, at Last: 1907

Alfred Lord Tennyson was the laureate of wishful thinking and the favorite poet of Lee de Forest. In the 1890s de Forest copied passages from *In Memoriam:* not only " 'T is better to have loved and lost / Than never to have loved at all" (section 27) but also some less notorious lines. Section 54 reflects Tennyson's desperate optimism:

> I can but trust that good shall fall
> At last—far off—at last, to all,
> And every winter change to spring.

In his journal de Forest recorded those lines, and in his heart he registered their theme. Most of his life would be one long winter interrupted only by false harbingers of spring. In 1900 de Forest rejoiced that "at last, *at last*" he was headed toward "success!" In 1907 he imagined a future "when at last I *shall* have made my dreams come true, & shall *at last* have really come into my own." In 1953, when he was eighty years old, he wrote to a bookshop in Los Angeles, seeking a volume of Tennyson's poems.[1]

After leaving American De Forest Wireless Telegraph, the thirty-three-year-old inventor helped organize a new company in the spring of 1907. Convinced by now that the human voice rather than dots and dashes rode the electromagnetic wave of the future, he called the firm the De Forest Radio Telephone Co. Later that year it was reorganized and renamed the Radio Telephone Co., with James Dunlop Smith, formerly one of Abraham White's best salesmen, as president.[2]

As the name of the new company suggests, radio in those early days was conceived of primarily as a substitute for the telephone—a means of private, point-to-point communication. De Forest, however, also recognized the possibilities of transmitting messages meant for no particular person but for the multitudes. Indeed, he may have been the first to apply the term *broadcast* to radio. From his Parker Building laboratory in the early months of 1907 he sent "synthetic" (electrically produced) music over the airwaves, noting in his journal that the music was "created in largess, scattered broadcast," and feeling happy "to distribute sweet melody broad-cast over the city & sea."[3]

In 1909 he "broadcast" an appeal for woman suffrage by Harriot Stanton Blatch—possibly, as he later claimed, the world's first taste of radio propaganda. Although the scarcity of radio receivers made the immediate audience tiny, newspaper coverage of the event brought welcome publicity for the company and the cause. In 1910 de Forest made more headlines by toting his radio apparatus to the Metropolitan Opera House and sending the voice of Enrico Caruso through the ether.[4]

From 1907 to 1909 de Forest enjoyed a modicum of commercial success. Late in 1907 the Radio Telephone Co. installed wireless apparatus on ships of the U.S. Navy before they embarked on a round-the-world cruise. (The sets did not work well, but de Forest blamed that on the haste with which they were installed and with which the Navy operators were trained.) According to radio archivist and historian G. H. Clark, de Forest and his company had more impact on early navy wireless than did any other man or company. His Radio Telephone Co. also built two stations for the U.S. Signal Corps and four for the Italian government. Meanwhile it manufactured and sold radio receivers to the amateur public.[5]

By transmitting music and speeches, de Forest doubtless did much to promote the nascent broadcasting industry, but it was in the quiet of his laboratory that he made his greatest contribution to radio. Late in 1906, while trying to develop a new detector of wireless signals, he invented the three-electrode vacuum tube (triode), which sober and meticulous historians have called "the most important single invention in the history of wireless" (W. Rupert Maclaurin) and even "one of the pivotal inventions of the twentieth century" (Hugh Aitken). By inserting a third electrode (called the "grid" because it was a wire bent back and forth so as to resemble a gridiron) between the cathode and the anode inside a vacuum tube, de Forest produced a device that detected and slightly strengthened incoming signals. In the form it took in 1906, the "Audion," as de Forest called it, was only a minor invention, just another detector. However, after the triode had undergone several important modifications, it would not only magnify signals enormously but also oscillate, producing a signal of its own. Thus it could be used as an amplifier or a transmitter.

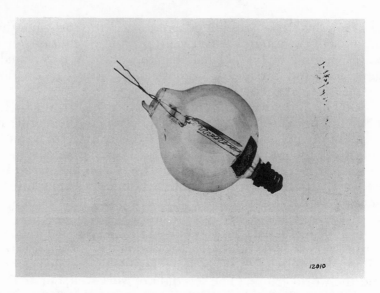

De Forest Audion, the triode vacuum tube, ca. 1913. Note the third electrode (grid) between the cathode (filament) and anode (plate). De Forest got the tube from Ambrose Fleming and the vacuum from AT&T, but the crucial third electrode was all his. Photo courtesy of AT&T Archives.

The improved triode was to become an essential element in radio technology and in the electronics industry generally.[6]

The improvements on the triode, however, were in the future. In 1907, when de Forest applied for a patent on the triode, it was not at all clear what use, if any, the device would have. Nor was it altogether apparent whether the triode was a fundamental improvement over earlier devices—a major invention—or merely something derived from them. The murkiness surrounding the triode's origin has not been entirely dispersed by historical investigation in the subsequent decades. Instead the story often has been obfuscated by claims and counterclaims stemming from the pride of rival inventors, the profit-seeking of corporations, the prejudice of biographers, the subtle nationalism of historians, and, most basically, the confusion inherent in the modern process of invention. The role of Lee de Forest in that story is not easy to discern.

Illustrating the difficulty in assigning credit for an invention to any one person, an analysis of de Forest's contribution to the vacuum tube must begin with Thomas Edison. In the early 1880s, Edison was studying electric lamps containing horseshoe-shaped carbon filaments, and he noticed that the lamps gradually blackened with use. However, he also noticed a fine streak along one side of the bulb, in the plane of the filament, where the dark deposit was much reduced. It seemed that particles of some kind were being emitted in straight lines from one leg of the filament, scattered across the inner surface of the bulb, but blocked by the other leg, thus creating a thin line—a white shadow—on the blackened bulb. Testing revealed that the shadow was being cast by the leg of the filament connected to the positive pole of the supply circuit. Edison then inserted into the bulb a second electrode, a metal plate, between the legs of the filament, connecting the plate first to the positive leg of the filament, then to the negative one. When this second, "cold" electrode was wired to the positive leg, a current flowed across the space between them; but when the plate was connected to the negative leg, the current did not flow. Particles moved from the heated filament to the cold plate, but only when the plate was positively charged, which meant that the particles must carry a negative charge. But since J. J. Thomson would not discover the electron until 1897 and O. W. Richardson would not publish his theory of electron emission until 1902, Edison did not know what the particles were, nor why they behaved as they did. Nevertheless, he applied for a patent on his device in 1883 and received it the following year.[7]

In subsequent years several inventors followed up on Edison's researches. William Preece, chief engineer of the British General Post Office, duplicated Edison's experiments, made quantitative measures, and coined the term "Edison effect." Further work was done by Preece's friend, J. Ambrose Fleming. Fleming, a professor of engineering at University College, London, was an academician with a practical bent, serving as a consultant to the Edison Electric Light Co. of London (appointed 1882) and the Marconi Wireless Telegraph Co. (appointed 1899). Keeping well informed of the latest developments in theoretical physics, electric lamps, and wireless, Fleming was uniquely situated to put vacuum tubes to work in radio.

Like Edison, Fleming was intrigued by what he called the "molecular shadow" produced in bulbs, and he presented a series of papers on that subject between 1883 and 1896. In the last of these, he stated that the current in a two-electrode tube (diode) flowed from the filament to the plate but not the other way: "a negative discharge can take place from hot to cold but never *vice versa*." By observing that the conductivity in the diode was unidirectional, he made clear his understanding that the tube rectified alternating current, that is, converted alternating current to direct current by permitting the current to pass in only one direction. Fleming did not yet propose any use for this feature, but he would have it in mind later when he worked on wireless.[8]

In 1904 Fleming, as technical adviser to the Marconi Co., was trying to develop a new kind of detector of wireless telegraph signals. Partly because he was going deaf, he wanted something that would record signals in visible form rather than receive them as sounds. The best existing device for visibly indicating current was a "mirror galvanometer," but this operated only on direct current, not on the alternating current produced by the oscillation of wireless transmitters. Fleming, however, recalled his earlier work with electric lamps. The Edison Effect bulb had rectified currents at low frequencies; if it would do the same at the high frequencies used by Marconi, then it could convert wireless signals into direct current and make feasible the use of the galvanometer. Retrieving some old Edison Effect lamps that he had stored in a cabinet, Fleming made the experiment, and it worked. "I have found a method," he reported to Marconi, "of rectifying electrical oscillations . . . so that I can detect them with an ordinary mirror galvanometer . . . This opens up a wide field for work, as I can now measure exactly the effect of the transmitter." Fleming gave the name "Oscillation Valve" to the Edison Effect lamp used this way, because it received wireless oscillations and allowed the current to pass in only one direction, just as a hydraulic valve allows water to go only one way. Quickly, however, the device became known as the Fleming Valve. Fleming applied for a British patent in 1904 and received it in 1905.[9]

As historian Gerald Tyne has emphasized, however, Ambrose Fleming did not invent the Fleming Valve. What he did was to take Edison's lamp, put it to a novel use, and call it a valve.[10] But what gives Fleming a stronger claim to originality was his demonstrated understanding of how the valve operated, an understanding superior to that of Edison earlier and de Forest later.

Fleming's earliest valves had a vacuum no more complete than that in an ordinary light bulb: they contained residual gas. When the filament was heated, it excited the gas molecules, ionizing them; and it was the ions that conducted the electric current. However, Fleming gradually came to realize that there was a better way to get the job done: not through gas ionization but through pure electron emission from the filament. In his original patent application in 1904 Fleming called for the highest vacuum possible in the tube, suggesting that there might be no need for any gas. In 1905 he delivered a paper to the Royal Society of

London in which he made use of the newly minted word *electron,* showing he was aware of the latest theoretical breakthroughs by Thomson and Richardson. Finally, in 1906, he gave a paper explicitly explaining the operation of the valve in terms of modern electronic theory. At low vacuum, he said, the tube functioned through the conductivity of residual gas. But when the tube was highly evacuated and the anode received a positive potential, then the current flow consisted of the discharge of electrons from the cathode, with the heated filament serving not to excite the gas into ionization but to emit electrons directly. Moreover, Fleming showed, this pure electron emission was more efficient than gas ionization, so the valve functioned better when the vacuum was high.[11]

By 1906, then, Fleming was able to explain for the first time how the Edison Effect lamp/Fleming Valve worked. Far better than Edison, he understood what the device did and was. Edison invented it, but Fleming discovered it.

Meanwhile, on the other side of the Atlantic Ocean, Lee de Forest was trying to build a new detector for wireless telegraph signals. Since 1900 he had been attempting to detect currents in ionized gas and had relied on Bunsen burners to heat the gas into ionization. In 1906, however, when it occurred to him that his detector would be more stable if it were enclosed and the gas were heated without an open flame, de Forest started using a partially evacuated bulb with a hot filament that ionized the residual gas. This was the first of the devices that de Forest was to call the "Audion," though at this point it was a "two-electrode Audion," quite different in function and usefulness from the three-electrode one that would soon follow.

De Forest's diode, with an incandescent filament and a cold electrode, was notably similar to the Fleming Valve—a similarity noted by Fleming himself, patent attorneys for the company that employed him (Marconi), and historians of radio. To the end of his life, de Forest would maintain that the two-electrode Audion had evolved logically and solely from the gas-flame detector and had not been influenced in any way by Fleming's work. Faced with accusations that he had copied the Fleming Valve much as he previously had copied Fessenden's electrolytic detector, de Forest needed to fortify his position in patent litigation as well as defend his personal reputation for originality and honesty. He pointed out structural differences between the diode Audion and the valve, said that the two devices functioned differently, and denied even knowing of the valve before he invented the Audion.[12]

Recent historians, however, have found de Forest's debt to Fleming greater than de Forest ever acknowledged. Aitken concludes that the valve and the two-electrode Audion were functionally identical. Moreover, Tyne shows that de Forest had seen and used Fleming Valves well before he filed for a patent on the two-electrode Audion. Clifford D. Babcock, de Forest's assistant, had gone to glass manufacturer H. W. McCandless in late 1905, showed him a Fleming Valve, and ordered duplicates. De Forest then used these duplicates in his experiments. De Forest himself, in a patent application filed in December 1905, mentioned a rectifier described in a paper by Fleming. Thus it appears that learning of the valve had led de Forest to stop using an open flame to ionize gas and to use a filament in a glass envelope instead.[13]

Fleming's priority in this regard, however, does not diminish de Forest's principal claim to fame, the *three*-electrode vacuum tube. As Aitken has shown, Fleming and de Forest were working on different problems, thinking along different lines, and moving in different directions. Although the Fleming Valve and the de Forest diode were "practically indistinguishable" as physical artifacts, they had radically different intellectual histories.

> To Fleming what he had discovered was essentially a valve. It permitted electricity to flow in one direction but not in the other, and by virtue of that fact it was a rectifier and a detector of high-frequency currents. To de Forest it was essentially a relay—a means whereby a small current in the antenna circuit could control a larger reaction in the audio circuit.

Fleming was looking for a rectifier that would enable him to use the mirror galvanometer; when he discovered the valve, he had reached his goal and had little incentive to continue developing the instrument. De Forest's two-electrode Audion was much less successful, never working well enough as a detector to be practical: only one receiving set using the de Forest diode was ever sold. Therefore, de Forest needed to continue improving the Audion, and he ultimately did so by adding a third electrode.[14]

On 25 November 1906, de Forest ordered from manufacturer McCandless a new kind of tube, one with a third electrode interposed between the filament and the anode. To prevent this third electrode from blocking the passage of "particles" between the filament and the anode, de Forest specified that it consist of a wire instead of a solid plate. John Grogan, an assistant to McCandless, suggested that to create a greater surface drawing electrons from the filament, the wire be bent back and forth; and de Forest named this innovation the "grid." He then made this triode Audion into a detector by connecting the anode to an earphone and connecting the grid to an antenna for receiving wireless signals. The anode circuit carried a strong current produced by a battery; the grid circuit carried a weaker current produced by wireless signals. Located between the filament and the anode, the grid magnified the amplitude of the wireless signals by superimposing on them the current from the anode circuit. Thus the earphone received much louder sounds than would have been possible without the third electrode. De Forest began testing the new tube on 31 December, filed for a patent on 29 January 1907, and received it (No. 879,532) on 18 February 1908.[15]

The triode Audion worked; and, as Aitken has demonstrated, it worked in the way that De Forest always said it did—by controlling the flow of current in ionized gas, not in a vacuum. Although de Forest borrowed the physical apparatus of the Fleming Valve, he did not expropriate the electronic theory that Fleming was expounding by 1906. Instead de Forest continued to insist that residual gas in the tube was necessary for the Audion to function. The very name *Audion,* coined by de Forest's assistant Clifford Babcock, meant "audible ions"—showing how de Forest intended to use gas ionization to hear wireless signals. Consequently it would not be until after 1912, when engineers at AT&T and General Electric realized the need to evacuate the tube thoroughly, eliminating the gas and depending on pure electron emission from the filament, that the Audion would become powerful and durable enough to be widely used as an amplifier. Moreover, according to Aitken, de Forest's laboratory notebooks indicate no awareness of the triode's potential as a transmitter until 1912, when the idea had already occurred to other inventors. This tardiness would cost de Forest dearly.[16]

Nevertheless, his invention of the triode tube, his imaginative efforts in broadcasting, and his company's manufacture and sale of radio apparatus all brought him a long-desired taste of fame. In 1908 Marconi, the man whom he hoped someday to eclipse, said in an interview that his American rival was doing "great things" in wireless. When de Forest read this praise (in the Pottstown, Pennsylvania, *Ledger*), he was thrilled.[17]

In de Forest's checkered life, professional and romantic fortunes often followed the same pattern. At precisely the same time that he was inventing the triode, he turned his extramural attentions to the girl next door and discovered a New Woman. "A new Year, a new Era, a new Hope, has dawned upon my life," he wrote on the first day of 1907. "*At last, at last,* the weary search has ended." He had found his Golden Girl. Twenty-three-year-old Nora Stanton Blatch lived with her mother in the apartment next to the one de Forest shared with his mother and brother; and when Nora played the piano, the melody penetrated many walls. Before long, her music-loving neighbor was courting her seriously, even theatrically: slipping notes under her door and reciting verses to her (he called English-born Nora "Leonora" or "Eleonora," after a Poe subject).[18]

Beset by radio work and worries, De Forest thought that a woman's companionship offered him salvation. Ever since deciding to go to Sheffield Scientific School instead of Yale College, he had feared becoming "only" a scientist, a narrow-minded technician, without refinement and taste. In college and graduate school, while studying electromagnetism, he had found release with Emerson and Poe. In Chicago, while inventing a system of wireless telegraphy, he had acquired a liking for classical music (he took "unmeasured pleasure" in Berlioz's *Damnation of Faust*). Surrounded by coils, capacitors, and vacuum tubes, he now needed someone to teach him "how to be something *besides* an automaton." Hoping to be "a human being first—a Genius next," he begged Nora to bring music, poetry, and romance back into his life.[19]

The quest for the Golden Girl was over at last. Tall and robust, with a spiritual beauty "beyond a fleshly ideal," Nora was all that he had been looking for. Besides being well-educated, hard-working, and free-thinking, she shared de Forest's fondness for music and the out-of-doors. Finally, he said contentedly, "she commingles maidenly reserve with a whole-hearted frankness, mental gifts of a rare degree with all the glad enthusiasms of wholesome, healthful girlish nature."[20]

Foremost among those girlish glad enthusiasms was a devotion to women's rights. Nora Stanton Blatch was the daughter of suffragist Harriot Stanton Blatch and the granddaughter of Elizabeth Cady Stanton; she got her first name from the heroine of Ibsen's *A Doll's House*. Trained in civil engineering at Cornell University (where she, unlike de Forest, was elected to Sigma Xi), Nora worked for the New York City Board of Water Supply. Intelligent and independent, she lived up to her name, making it not only a record of history but also an instrument of prophecy.[21]

In January 1907, after becoming engaged to the inventor, Nora

Three generations of feminists, ca. 1887. Elizabeth Cady Stanton (center), Harriot Stanton Blatch (right), and the future Nora Blatch de Forest. Photo courtesy of Rhoda Barney Jenkins—architect, local leader of the National Organization for Women, and member of the fourth generation.

Left: Nora Blatch at Cornell University, 1905. Right: throwing quoits on the honeymoon cruise, 1908. On the back of the honeymoon photo de Forest, a believer in inherited characteristics, wrote of his bride: "There's a delicacy, alertness, refinement in that glance, that takes its source in more than one lifetime back." Photos courtesy of Rhoda Jenkins.

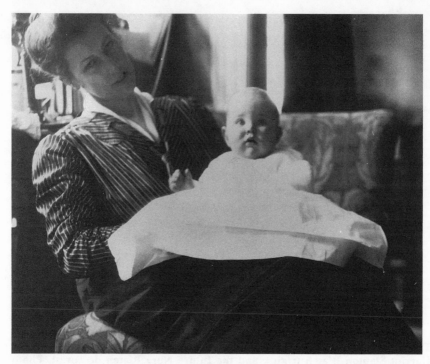

Nora and Harriot de Forest, 1909. By the time the baby was born, her parents were separated and on their way to a bitter divorce. Photo courtesy of Rhoda Jenkins.

The Horseback Crusade for woman suffrage, 1913. Left: Nora rides from town to town in upstate New York. Right: on the soapbox. Note the convertible culottes, which could be buttoned in front and back (to make a skirt) or along the inseams (to make trousers for riding). The personal is political. Photos courtesy of Rhoda Jenkins.

"The glad enthusiasms of wholesome healthful girlish nature." Intrepid Nora (left) tells a throng of men why women should vote. Photo courtesy of Rhoda Jenkins.

resolved to become familiar with his work. She was disillusioned
with her position at the Water Board, having observed that "the
whole interest seemed to focus on higher pay and doing as little
work as possible." She gladly quit her job and enrolled at Columbia University to study electricity under the noted inventor
Michael Pupin. Impressed by his fiancée's decision to forego her
career and "to entrust your energies, your hopes, your life-work
with my own," de Forest felt that he had found a "complete
companion."[22]

Between the engagement and the wedding, more than a year
elapsed. De Forest's divorce from Lucile Sheardown moved slowly
through the courts, and it was not until early in 1908 that he was
free to remarry. Meanwhile Nora's ardor had cooled. Beginning
to doubt the wisdom of the match, she considered calling it off. It
may have given her pause when her fiancé borrowed a thousand
dollars from her mother. De Forest reassured Nora, however; and
on 24 February 1908, they exchanged vows before a justice of the
peace in Greenwich, Connecticut. With Nora, as with Lucile two
years before, de Forest crossed the Atlantic for a honeymoon. But
love was truly lovelier the second time around. Although storms
swirled around the steamship, inside the newlyweds' cabin "blue
skies have ever prevailed, reflected from *her eyes.*" Now when de
Forest spoke of his *wife,* the word had meaning for him.[23]

After landing in Liverpool, the couple combined business with
pleasure. Besides admiring the sights of Europe, de Forest demonstrated his radio equipment to potential buyers. Nora also kept
busy. In London she joined a suffrage parade, marching through
Hyde Park and down Whitehall to the Houses of Parliament. De
Forest stood on the sidelines and applauded as she passed. He saw
no reason why women should not be allowed to vote, and he
admired the courage of the marchers.[24]

De Forest's support for women's equality, however, was incon-
sistent at best. On the one hand, he clung to early acquired ideas
of female inferiority. In his very first journal he copied a quotation that he attributed to the American Puritan poet Anne
Bradstreet: "Men can do best, and women know it well." A visit to
a Christian Science church in 1897 disgusted him with "*woman's*
superstition" and extirpated any "leanings toward the accordance
of equal rights to woman" that he may previously have had. While
joining the jingoes in 1898, de Forest said that "Peace efforts, like
many womanly missionary projects, are 'good,' but most awfully
foolish and unwise." Women provided necessary comfort and
support, but their judgment was not to be trusted.[25]

On the other hand, de Forest's peculiar "progressivism" did give him some of those "leanings" toward equal rights that Mary Baker Eddy inadvertently extinguished. In 1894 de Forest said that scientific research was sufficiently "lady-like" to provide employment for women, though he doubted that *married* women would have time to discover much. When asked in 1896 what woman's "proper sphere" was, he replied, "This terrestrial ball, as much of it as she can hold down." In 1897 he denounced St. Paul as "the cowardly defender of slavery and the despiser of women."[26]

Marriage to Nora Stanton Blatch would force de Forest to face the contradictions in his ideas about women. In 1896 he had said that what he admired most in a woman was "unconventionality of spirit within the bonds of true femininity"—thus demanding her freedom and at the same time forbidding it. Now, in 1907, the inventor said his fiancée typified "the new woman—noble & self-knowing—independent yet all-womanly, never the Doll of the 'Doll's House.'" Nora, however, was indeed Nora, more independent than "womanly." Years later her daughter Rhoda remembered her as someone who would not yield or compromise but must have her way. She was a perfect match for Lee de Forest—as in a boxing match.[27]

In June 1908 de Forest returned to New York, but his wife did not go with him. Instead she visited relatives in Basingstoke, England (her birthplace), then journeyed to Freiburg, Switzerland, where she studied a new type of capacitor. Not until the end of October did she rejoin her husband. When at last she sailed into New York harbor on board the ill-fated *Lusitania,* she unfurled a banner reading "Votes for Women."[28]

Less than a year after the honeymoon cruise, the marriage was on the rocks. One cause of the rapid disaffection was Nora's suspicion that the top officers of the Radio Telephone Co. were reckless and dishonest; Lee resented the slurs against his colleagues. A more important source of discord was professional rivalry within the family. Having switched from civil to electrical engineering, Nora gave herself wholly to the new vocation. Although Lee had originally been flattered by Nora's decision to follow him into his field of study, he soon found that he preferred her companionship in some place other than the lab. While he wanted her to provide him with the music and poetry of life, she wanted to supervise operations at the capacitor factory. Arguments were frequent and bitter. In August 1908 Nora had told her husband that "I know I'd never tire of living with you, nay not for 1000 years," but early the next year she moved out of the house.[29]

To make her departure all the more exasperating, she was

The inventor behind the wheel of his first car, a new Chalmers-Detroit, in 1909. The prestigious Chalmers was the choice of Rockefellers and Vanderbilts. In the back seat are (from left) the baby's "Nurse Cox," Nora de Forest, and Harriot Blatch. Photo courtesy of Rhoda Jenkins.

pregnant when she left. De Forest considered the birth of his first child momentous; but when a girl was born on 19 June 1909, he was not present and was informed by telephone. The baby was named Harriot Stanton de Forest.[30]

In the next two years de Forest visited his firstborn often, proving himself a doting father. He delighted in tickling her with wisps of cotton, kissing her cheeks and hair, entertaining her with marionettes and mechanical dolls. It thrilled him when she first learned to say *Papa* and *de Forest*. "When I felt this little miracle of Baby-perfectness, of love, and all adorable qualities, so close to me, so trusting in me, growing so dear to me," he said, "all the cares and ambitions of the whole world would disappear, and I live like my child, uplifted to a new world, where all is good and all is *Now*."[31]

Except when his work called him away from New York, de Forest tried to see Harriot for at least one hour each day. Cherish-

The father and the firstborn, ca. 1911. De Forest visited Harriot often, doted on her, and could not understand why her mother did not spend more time with her. Photo courtesy of Perham Foundation.

ing these moments, he wondered how Nora could continue working as an engineer and social reformer, how any mother could bear going to a lab or office when such an amiable baby remained at home. Calling Harriot "motherless," he believed that only he and the hired nurse provided the child with its necessary ration of affection. Over the years, de Forest tried to understand Nora's apparent deficiency of mother love. In 1911 he blamed it on conditioning: "the unnatural, unloving, unsexed manner of her bringing up." Given the education and ambitions of a man, she lacked tenderness toward her offspring. Sometime later, however, de Forest considered the hypothesis that motherliness was biologically determined. Reading a Rockefeller Foundation study on the ductless glands, he learned that a female rat which at first is indifferent to offspring offered to her for adoption will eagerly adopt the baby rats after she is injected with a pituitary hormone. In the margin of the report the inventor drew a significant conclusion: "*Mother love* determined by chemical reactions."[32]

Absence from Nora did not make de Forest's heart grow fonder. In June 1911, more than two years after separating, he explained to his mother what had ruined his marriage. Nora, he said, had shown him no sympathy. When they had disagreed, she had never met him halfway, "nor attempted in any of a hundred feminine ways to win a man to her will, by those charming cajoleries (which she holds in unspeakable disdain) which all men expect of woman." Her scientific work, he said, had made her "all mentality and calculating ambition" with hardly a thought for anything else. Although once he had believed her to have a spiritual beauty "beyond a fleshly ideal," he now found her appearance disgusting. Stoop-shouldered and flat-chested, she wore a panama hat three years out of fashion and, what was worse, a *blue* skirt with *tan* shoes and stockings! The horrified husband concluded that she was a "typical suffragette . . . Man-hating, sexless, unfeminine, ambitious to fill man's place, to surpass him in his own sphere."[33]

Needless to say, relations between the couple were not cordial. De Forest complained that Nora would not let him see Harriot often enough, nor provide him with news and photographs of the child. "Fortunate for you," he told his wife, "that you early turned atheist and abandoned hope of immortality, else by night some half-realization of your crimes against a fellow-being might shake your warped soul with dread." Each meeting between de Forest and Nora was a struggle, sometimes with Harriot the viciously contested prize. While the father coaxed the baby to say "I love

Papa," the mother taught her "Votes for Women." De Forest told the press that Harriot Stanton Blatch had even offered him five thousand dollars if he would surrender his rights to his daughter, but he had refused. He warned all young men against marrying into families where there is "suffrage in the blood."[34]

Late in 1911 the de Forests were divorced. For Lee, the crack-up of his second marriage was only one of his worries.[35]

In the spring of 1909, not long after Nora had left de Forest's Manhattan apartment, James Dunlop Smith tendered his resignation as president of the Radio Telephone Co. As he did so, he revealed that twenty thousand shares of stock recently sold had been his own, not the company's, and that the company was nearly broke. Now de Forest wished that he had heeded what he called Nora's "womanly intuitions" regarding Smith's management. However, rather than bring a lawsuit against the former president, thereby destroying what public confidence the company still enjoyed, de Forest and the remaining directors chose to reorganize the firm. Radio Telephone was merged with two other companies, forming the North American Wireless Corp. Although engineering and commercial activities were cut back, the work went on. De Forest spent most of the spring and summer of 1910 on the West Coast, installing radio sets on Navy transports.[36]

The year 1911 was another nadir in the inventor's life. With both his marriage and his company shipwrecked, he lamented that he was *born to be robbed*—robbed of many of the best of college associations; robbed of the best of social influences; . . . robbed of the fruits of my years of toil (twice robbed there)— robbed of my wife (twice robbed)." Brooding over the disasters that had repeatedly befallen him, he concluded that there must be something wrong with his character. His tragic flaw, he decided, was an inability to keep from being "defrauded and despoiled." The cause of his misery, he believed, was an excessive trust in his fellow human beings.[37]

The North American Wireless Corp. did not prosper; and with the company sinking ever deeper into insolvency, de Forest abandoned ship. Having enjoyed his trip to California in 1910, he took a job the following year as an engineer with the Federal Telegraph Co. in Palo Alto. The relocation proved fortunate. After two decades in the chill of New England, the Midwest, and New York, de Forest reveled in the sun of the Golden State. Though his overexposed nose became "like a red sunset," he enjoyed swimming at Ocean Park. Hiking through the Sausalito Hills, he remembered the outdoor days of his childhood. De Forest liked everything about his new home, even the politics. After California had approved woman suffrage (which he still favored, despite his experience with one suffragist), he gave "Three *cheers for California—my* State—of Freedom and Progressiveness."[38]

Even in the state of freedom, however, one could be collared by the long arm of federal law. On 27 March 1912, two U.S. marshals showed up at de Forest's door with a warrant for his arrest. Two weeks earlier North American Wireless had gone bankrupt, and he and three other former officers of its predecessor, Radio Telephone, had been indicted by a grand jury in New York on charges of using the mails to defraud. The four were accused of deceiving prospective buyers of stock by saying that the company was paying dividends from the net profits of its commercial operations and by exaggerating the commercial value of the radio telephone. De Forest and company president Smith were also charged with planning to swindle potential buyers. De Forest admitted that improper methods had been used but claimed that he had not known of it at the time.[39]

Ten thousand dollars bail bond, procured by his California employers, saved de Forest from the indignity of going to jail, but the prosecution proved embarrassing nevertheless. Two days after his arrest, he issued a statement whose vehemence made it not altogether reassuring. "I'm *not* a crook," he said. Some of his associates apparently believed him. Twenty-nine members of his class at Sheffield contributed to a "De Forest Defense Fund," whose goal was to provide $2,500 for legal fees. As it turned out, however, the group could raise only $803.[40]

De Forest's case was not settled for two years, giving the inventor prolonged inconvenience and anxiety. He spent weeks preparing his defense, and in November 1913 he went on trial in New York. There the federal prosecutor added insult to injury. To convince the jury that the Radio Telephone Co. had misled the public as to the future profitability of radio, he ridiculed de Forest's inventions. Holding an Audion in his hand, the district attorney said that the tube was worthless, that it was "not even a good lamp." When the jury went out on the last day of December, the chagrined inventor heard the judge instruct the members that they must decide, among other things, whether the wireless telephone could ever be as useful as the defendants claimed. The deliberations stretched beyond midnight, and cheers from Times Square floated through the courtroom. As 1913 become history,

De Forest wondered whether all his years of work had gone for nothing.

At one o'clock in the morning of 1 January, the jury announced its verdict. James Dunlop Smith and another officer of the company were found guilty on two counts and sent to the federal penitentiary. Lee de Forest and a fourth officer were found not guilty. Rejoicing that "the 'hoodoo year' is past," the inventor began 1914 with a resurgence of enthusiasm.[41]

He had reason for optimism. Since 1911 he had enjoyed a steadily rising measure of success in both love and work. By 1914 he had a new wife and the beginnings of a new fortune—his third of each.

The wife was Mary Mayo, a buxom singer from Brooklyn. De Forest first saw her in October 1912, when she sang soprano in the chorus of a comedy called "The Quaker Girl." With typical alacrity he married her on 23 December of the same year. A month later the ecstatic agnostic composed a prayer entitled "Mary Mayo de Forest":

> Dear God, teach me each night to face the west
> Sending aloft, because I am so blest
> My heart's thanksgiving when the day is done![42]

Professionally de Forest prospered also. Employed by Federal Telegraph, he addressed himself to the needs of the company, inventing in 1912 a "diplex" system of telegraphy which allowed two stations to transmit to each other simultaneously over a single wire. But the company did not narrowly restrict the inventor's energies. It allowed him to work on whatever interested him, and what interested him most was the Audion. Trying to increase amplification, de Forest in July 1912 arranged the tubes in what he called a "cascade," with the output of one triode becoming the input of another. Because each triode amplified signals about three times, three of them in cascade had an amplification factor of twenty-seven—a considerable improvement. But de Forest was on the verge of an even more important discovery. In August 1912 he connected the output circuit of an Audion to its own input circuit, instead of to a second Audion's. In so doing, he laid his claim to inventing the first "regenerative" or "feedback" circuit, which by recycling energy could magnify signals prodigiously. Moreover, when the feedback was sufficient, the regenerating triode would produce oscillations, a sustained alternating current, and thus could be used as a transmitter instead of an amplifier.[43]

Unfortunately, however, the inventor did not realize what he had done, a failing that was to cost him dearly in time, money, and reputation. Radio historian Tom Lewis credits de Forest with producing "a regeneration circuit of sorts, but of audio, not high frequency waves." Evidence proving de Forest achieved anything more than that, says Lewis, is "insubstantial in the extreme." De Forest understood so little of the potential of regeneration that he failed to copy the notes of his supposedly crucial August 1912 experiment, failed to explain regeneration technically, failed to make use of its oscillating feature, and as late as 1915 stated in print that oscillation did not depend on regeneration. Most telling, he did not apply for a patent on the regenerative circuit until 1915. That was late. In 1913 a graduate assistant at Columbia University, E. Howard Armstrong, delivered a paper about a regenerative circuit he had developed. In 1914 he received a patent on the same.[44]

For the next two decades de Forest and Armstrong engaged in what economic historian W. Rupert Maclaurin has called "the most controversial litigation in radio history." De Forest challenged Armstrong's priority, but federal courts twice upheld the younger man. Although de Forest sold his feedback rights to AT&T in 1917, the legal battle went on. In 1924 and 1927 federal courts reversed the previous decisions and awarded priority to de Forest. In 1928 the U.S. Supreme Court confirmed him as the inventor of regeneration, but in 1933 Armstrong won a new challenge in the Circuit Court of Appeals. It was not until a second Supreme Court decision in 1934, written by Justice Benjamin Cardozo, that de Forest achieved a definitive victory in court.[45]

But what the lawyers gave, the engineers took away. The Institute of Radio Engineers (in 1934), the Franklin Institute (1941), and the American Institute of Electrical Engineers (1942) all deplored the court decision and recognized Armstrong as the true inventor of feedback. As for de Forest, he received numerous awards from scientific societies for inventing the three-electrode tube but none for the regenerative circuit.[46]

While engaged in research, de Forest did not neglect the commercial side of invention. In October 1912 he offered to sell to the American Telephone & Telegraph Co. the right to use the Audion to amplify voice transmission over wires. The resoundingly named John Stone Stone, a respected technical consultant who was a friend of both de Forest and John J. Carty, chief engineer and vice president of AT&T, served as an intermediary between the inventor and the company. Through Stone, de Forest asked $100,000 for the patent rights, then waited impatiently while the company's engineers and attorneys evaluated the proposition. The AT&T group understood that the triode had great potential as a telephone "repeater" (amplifier) and was likely to become an essential element in long-distance telephony. Unfortunately, however, they found complications.[47]

The technical evaluation of de Forest's Audion was the responsibility of the Western Electric Co., the manufacturing subsidiary of AT&T. One of the newest members of Western Electric's research branch was Dr. Harold D. Arnold, who had just finished studying the new electronics under Robert A. Millikan at the University of Chicago. When Arnold examined the Audion, he recognized both its defects and its promise. The tube's filament was short-lived and required frequent readjustment. The internal elements were flimsy. Most important, the residual gas in the tube made it lose amplification and create unwanted noise when it was operated at the high level of input used in telephony. Still, Arnold realized that the Audion would amplify satisfactorily once it was thoroughly evacuated, and the other problems could be solved by teams of specialists in Western Electric's research laboratory. Therefore, Arnold was impressed by the "wonderful possibilities of that third electrode operation" and believed that the phone company could use it to make a practical amplifier.[48]

More worrisome for AT&T was the report from its legal department. The Radio Telephone and North American Wireless companies held rights to the Audion, and de Forest was not the only party claiming the assets of those two defunct companies. Moreover, there remained the question of whether the Audion was an infringement on the patent for the Fleming Valve, which now belonged to the powerful Marconi interests. If AT&T were to use the Audion, it would inevitably become subject to major lawsuits. The phone company took no precipitous action.[49]

Meanwhile, in May 1913, de Forest left Federal Telegraph and went back to New York. Hired by a group of businessmen interested in talking motion pictures, the inventor went to work on a system of recording sound on a steel wire that could be synchronized with film. Confident of the future, he and Mary moved into a made-to-order house on the Hudson River at Spuyten Duyvil, a house that he named "Riverlure—Where Dreams Come True." The dreams did come true, but not until after more rest-

less nights. Only a few months after de Forest returned to New
York, his employers ran out of money to sponsor research and to
pay his salary. Settled in a big new home filled with furniture
bought on the installment plan, de Forest had to pawn his watch
and his wife's wedding ring in order to eat. As he sat on the
veranda in the evenings, watching steamboats ply their way up the
river and listening to Mary play the piano, he wondered what
surprises the future still held. It was at about this time that he met
Sidney Meyers.[50]

There is some question about Meyers' role in the ensuing patent
negotiations between de Forest and AT&T. According to John
Stone Stone, the company asked Stone to withdraw as de Forest's
representative and allow the company to talk directly with de
Forest. Stone and de Forest agreed to this, Stone told a journalist
in 1941, and the company then sent Meyers, an attorney, to
arrange the sale. In de Forest's autobiography published in 1950,
however, there is no mention of the inventor's agreeing to a
change in negotiating procedures and personnel. Instead he says
that while awaiting word from AT&T, he was approached by
Meyers, who introduced himself as the agent for some anonymous clients, expressly denying any connection to the phone
company. Meyers, says de Forest, offered fifty thousand dollars
for the Audion rights—only half of what de Forest had been
asking from AT&T. However, ten months had passed since he
had made his proposal, and he feared that the company was not
interested after all. Therefore he sold the Audion rights to
Meyers and his assignees. Only later, he says, did he discover that
those nameless clients were Messrs. AT&T, and he lamented that
he had been "robbed" again.[51]

Whether or not he was swindled out of fifty thousand dollars,
the other fifty thousand made the penurious inventor feel like a
million bucks. Late in 1913, even while being tried for fraud, he
organized a new enterprise, the Radio Telephone & Telegraph
Co. The stock of the new outfit was offered in exchange for the
stocks and bonds of the old Radio Telephone and North American Wireless companies, and de Forest was in business again.[52]

In the coming decade de Forest's financial fortunes reached
their apex. Swamped with orders from the Allied armies, his new
company made large profits from the manufacture and sale of
radio equipment. Perhaps even more profitable was the sale of
patent rights. AT&T had already purchased the right to use the
triode for boosting transmission through telephone wires; but in

1914, somewhat belatedly, the company realized the usefulness of the triode for *wireless* telephony, that is, radio. As early as 1909 AT&T's chief engineer had written a memorandum suggesting the potential of wireless and emphasizing the importance of a "repeater" to amplify voice transmissions:

> While this branch of the art seems at present to be rather remote in its prospect of success, a most powerful impetus would be given to it if a suitable telephone repeater were available. Whoever can supply and control the necessary telephone repeater will exert a dominating influence in the art of wireless telephony when it is developed.

By 1914 AT&T was prepared to spend money in pursuit of a "dominating influence" in this promising new art. To de Forest's company, Radio Telephone & Telegraph, AT&T paid $90,000 for certain rights for radio signalling. Three years later Western Electric, the AT&T subsidiary, bought virtually all the remaining rights to the triode, leaving de Forest's company only the non-transferable right to manufacture tubes for sale to amateurs. The price paid by Western Electric was a handsome $50,000 plus dividends of $1.45 for each share of Radio Telephone & Telegraph stock, of which de Forest held almost 120,000 shares. "I have at last reached a safe & secure resting place," he observed after closing the deal with Western Electric. "No more shall I, as twice before (once in 1906 and again in 1910) see my castle of achievement crumble like a house of cards." In January 1919 the stockholders of Radio Telephone & Telegraph voted a return of capital assets, which netted de Forest a little over a hundred thousand dollars.[53]

While inventing, manufacturing, and selling radio equipment, de Forest continued his old pastime, broadcasting. In November 1916 he began transmitting music nightly from his plant in the Bronx, interspersing Columbia Gramophone records with sales pitches for de Forest radio apparatus. On election eve of that year, he made what may have been the first radio news broadcast, reading bulletins from the New York *American*. At 11 P.M., before returns in the West had been counted, the lifelong Republican, sometime New Yorker, and eternal optimist happily announced that Charles Evans Hughes had defeated Woodrow Wilson for the presidency.[54]

Wartime precautions silenced de Forest's transmitter in 1917 and 1918, but the following year he began broadcasting from Manhattan. Vaughn De Leath came to his station regularly and provided song and patter for that early day radio audience. Not everyone, however, was amused. In 1920 Uncle Sam ordered an end to de Forest's broadcasting, saying that it interfered with Navy and commercial radio telephone communication and that "there is no room in the ether for entertainment." Three decades later de Forest was still bitter about this decision. He was convinced that had he been permitted to continue broadcasting in New York, "that franchise and the fame which would ever after have attached thereto would unquestionably be worth today many millions of dollars."[55]

While the federal government denied him future fame and fortune, scientific and commercial rivals tried to deprive him of past achievement. As the AT&T legal staff had foreseen, his triode patents were insecure, and between 1914 and 1943 they underwent many challenges. The inventor's primary antagonist turned out to be Ambrose Fleming, the Englishman who in 1904 had patented the two-electrode vacuum tube, which served as a detector of wireless signals and which probably gave de Forest the idea of using a glass bulb to enclose gas in his own detector and using an incandescent filament to heat the gas. While de Forest's addition of a third electrode was revolutionary, the Audion still depended on apparatus covered under the broad Fleming patent. As early as 1906 Fleming had claimed that the triode was only a minor modification of the valve and not a genuine invention. In October 1914 the American Marconi Co., which in 1905 had bought Fleming's patent, brought suit against Radio Telephone & Telegraph for infringement. De Forest, noting that Marconi used a third electrode in its tubes, countered by suing Marconi for infringing on the Audion patent.[56]

The litigation produced a stalemate. In September 1916 a U.S. district court ruled the De Forest company guilty of infringing the Fleming Valve and forbade it to manufacture triodes without the Marconi company's consent. Meanwhile, however, Marconi admitted infringing the de Forest Audion patent and agreed (out of court) not to manufacture triodes without de Forest's consent. In effect, Marconi owned the anode and the cathode, de Forest owned the grid, and neither side could make a whole triode without the permission of the other. In 1917 and 1918 neither party would grant that permission, but it made no difference: both were granted immunity from injunctions in order to fulfill government contracts. After the war a modus vivendi was worked out, with a third party producing tubes for both the Marconi and de Forest companies. This arrangement was profitable but short-lived.

In October 1919 the General Electric Co. bought control of the American Marconi Co. and turned Marconi's assets over to a new firm, the Radio Corporation of America, with which GE exchanged all patent rights. In July 1920 RCA negotiated a cross-licensing agreement with AT&T, which previously had purchased rights to de Forest's triode; and in June 1921 the Westinghouse Electric Co. also signed the agreement. Under this arrangement AT&T gave RCA the right to manufacture triodes; RCA gave the right to GE and Westinghouse; GE and Westinghouse made the triodes, put them into radios, and sold the radios to RCA; RCA sold the radios to the public; and nobody had to buy anything from the Radio Telephone & Telegraph Co. of Lee de Forest. Fleming's patent on the diode expired in 1922, leaving de Forest's company free to manufacture and sell triodes; but in the coming years the company would not be able to make tubes as well or as cheaply as those of the AT&T-RCA-GE-Westinghouse combine. Radio Telephone & Telegraph went into receivership in about 1926, was revived in 1928, flourished for a few years, but in 1933 went into its final receivership, with its assets being bought up by RCA. The small business, the independent producer, was done in by competition from big corporations and by cooperation among them.

Yet de Forest obtained satisfaction of a sort. In 1943 the Supreme Court ruled that Fleming's patent on the diode had covered discoveries made by earlier inventors and therefore had been invalid all along. At last, long after his Audion patents had expired, de Forest held unchallenged title to the invention of the three-electrode vacuum tube. It was no small claim to fame.[57]

During his middle years, de Forest continued the pursuit of fame that he had begun in his youth. He seldom missed an opportunity to make his name known to the public, and he resented it if anyone denied or ignored his achievement. In 1915 he reacted angrily when the AT&T exhibit at the Panama-Pacific International Exposition at San Francisco boasted of sending telephone messages across the continent but did not mention using triodes as amplifiers. When AT&T gave visitors a brochure entitled "The Story of a Great Achievement: Telephone Communication from Coast to Coast," de Forest responded by distributing pamphlets entitled "The Story of a Great Achievement: Which

Made Telephone Communication from Coast to Coast Possible."
Two years later, when de Forest sold AT&T the right to develop
transatlantic radio telephony with the Audion, he vowed to "see if
publicity can not be so engineered that the world shall know
whose inventions made it possible." Public relations extended
beyond the professional sphere. On 6 January 1918, after ten days
of sub-zero temperatures, de Forest walked across the frozen
Hudson River opposite 230th Street, and newspaper coverage of
the lark provided him with the desired notoriety.[58]

During the Great War de Forest was in the papers often, leading
the cheers for the Allies. In January 1916 he appeared before the
Engineers Club of Trenton, New Jersey, to debate the issue of
preparedness with Navy Secretary Josephus Daniels. While
Daniels assured the engineers that the American military was
ready to fight if necessary, de Forest condemned the armed forces'
present state and called for universal military training. Moreover,
de Forest deplored President Wilson's attempt to conciliate Germany, calling it a sacrifice of honor. Americans pusillanimously
worshipped the dollar, he said, and would take any opportunity
for trade, even with Germans. In May 1916 he wrote to the New
York *Sun*, urging the election of a president who would tolerate
no such stains on the national honor, Theodore Roosevelt. The
old hero thanked de Forest for writing the letter.[59]

The inventor's attitude toward war was much as it had been in
1898. Those who opposed entry were "craven," he said in September 1916, for the Allies represented "humanity & civilization."
Two years later, after American involvement had helped bring
Germany near defeat, he envisioned the last campaign as Armageddon. "If the stubborn will of the brutish nation is still un-
broken," he swore, "five million stalwart fighting men will grimly
rejoice as they gird tighter their sword for the last, exhilarating
blow for justice!" At age forty-three, Lee de Forest was too old to
buckle on the armor, but he could advance the crusade in other
ways. In December 1916, as he negotiated with Western Electric
for the sale of patent rights, he vowed that if the deal went
through, he would make "a genuine sacrifice" for his country. But
the sacrifice would be money, not life nor limb. "This stupid
nation richly deserves the punishment she invites," he said. "I'm
sure I would not be willing to fight & die for such a people as ours
have shown ourselves to be—a characterless, incohesive goulash."[60]

Western Electric did buy the patent rights; de Forest did contribute five thousand dollars to the American Defense Society;

and the "incohesive goulash" did finally go to war, much to the inventor's delight. After watching a Red Cross parade in May 1918, he noted that "America is a new & far nobler land since this war began to awaken our soul." To support the cause, he bought a five thousand dollar Liberty Bond, and his wife sang in a musicale for the benefit of blinded French soldiers.[61]

Mary Mayo de Forest did not sing often anymore. In the years since her marriage, she had neglected her voice and her career and had taken heavily to drink. The cause of her alcoholism can only be surmised. In 1918 Mary was bedridden with rheumatism; alcohol may have been an anodyne for physical pain that she had endured for years. Whatever its cause, her drunkenness helped destroy her marriage. By December 1916 Lee de Forest found that her drinking was bringing him to despair, killing his spirit, making him "a dead man alive." The following month he resolved not to suffer anymore for his wife's sake. "The world's too large!" he said.[62]

In October 1918 business called him to Europe, and he made the most of the adventure. In Paris when the peace was announced, he and a "charming brown-eyed grisette" enjoyed "to our fullest capacity that historic and never-to-be-forgotten celebration of the Night of the first Armistice Day." Years later he would happily recall the bottles of wine, the Folies Bergere, and the subsequent events of the night which he discreetly covered with a "hazy veil of obsolescence and forget-me-nots."[63]

De Forest had a grand time in France. He attended the opera regularly and in his less sedate moments resumed the pranks of his college days. With the help of his patent lawyer, he stole an American flag from a bank in Paris; and at the theater he joined the raucous American Expeditionary Forces in telling the French "just who the hell it was who made the World Safe for Democracy." De Forest studied the French language diligently, producing (or perhaps reproducing) a poem that showed ingenuity if not proficiency:

Couráge

Par soldats Francais c'est reconte:
"En Cabinet des aisement
Where filled and locked was every place
A stranger rushed in urgent has/e [sic]
(Too pressed in fact to add the t
For he had more to do than P).

Mary Mayo. De Forest met her in October 1912, married her on 23 December, and on New Year's Eve urged "My Dear Little Wife" to "Write me today, *if you love me*." Photo courtesy of Perham Foundation.

The ancient dame, la charge des affairs,
Distressed to see him rush and swear
Speeds silent listening by each seat,
Tres jealous, crying 'Tout a suite.'
Then, just in time to save the day,
'Courage, Monsieur, J'entend papier.' "[64]

While romping in Paris, de Forest did not give up on the woman back home. He wrote frequent letters begging her to resume her musical training and coaxing her to get back on the wagon and stay there. When he returned to New York in January 1919, he found that his preachments seemed to have worked. During his absence Mary had endured the "unspeakable agony" of crippling rheumatism aggravated by loneliness, a "hard experience" that had made her "a different girl—so sweet and fond, so affectionate and considerate—that a new joy has entered my heart." Rejoicing over this miraculous conversion, de Forest took his wife to California for a second honeymoon, where they hiked, rode horseback, and took motor trips (Mary's rheumatism seems to have cleared up temporarily). After returning to New York, Mary looked forward to resuming her singing career. She practiced hard, gave concerts in Central Park and at Columbia University, and tried out (unsuccessfully) with the Met.[65]

More felicity lay ahead, for the man of the family at least. After years of barrenness, Mary was pregnant. Since his divorce from Nora, de Forest had seen little of his daughter Harriot, but now gestating in Mary's womb was a child that would be wholly and everlastingly his. As the months flipped by, de Forest impatiently awaited the arrival of "Lee Junior," imagining a bright future for the boy. When a baby was born on 30 September 1919, de Forest felt "the thrill of parenthood—so long denied."[66]

The child was something of a disappointment: it was a girl. But after getting over the first shock, De Forest welcomed her, cradling her in his arms, letting her tiny fingers squeeze his. Mary suggested that the newcomer be named Lea, but de Forest objected that "*sometime* there might be a brother named Lee!—& that would be confusing." So, going back to a favorite name from Poe, they named the girl Eleanor.

It had not been an easy birth. Mary, with a body already tortured by rheumatism, endured "terrific spasms of pain" for more than a day. When the baby finally emerged, it was badly bruised; and after the delivery, the doctor had to cut away afterbirth that clung to the mother's uterus. For Mary Mayo de Forest, childbirth was an ordeal that she would not gladly repeat. Nevertheless, once the child was born, Mary showed it ample "mother yearning," giving it "overwhelming love." To Lee de Forest's satisfaction, moreover, Mary's affection did not go out only to her offspring. "Already," he said, "Mary loves me, the father of her child, more deeply than she has ever done before." Certain that the baby would draw the parents closer together, he felt joy as he realized "that at last, there is no gulf, new or widening, to separate me from my wife & my child!" Remembering how he had been robbed of Lucile, Nora, and Harriot, he looked forward to contentment when Mary and Eleanor returned from the hospital:

And now, after another week of loneliness, they will come back to this house—at last a *home*—to "Riverlure, Where Dreams Come True"! Now, at last, I can begin to live![67]

5

I Can Steel My Heart: 1926

In the 1920s the inventor's world began to seem crowded. When he had begun his radio work two decades earlier, he had been a pioneer. But now, with corporations like Western Electric, General Electric, Westinghouse, and RCA sending herds of research engineers into the field, de Forest looked for elbow room. Leaving radio behind, he sought a new application of the Audion amplifier, one that he could develop "largely by my own efforts" and without a "large corps of engineers backed by a gigantic business organization." Before long he found that application—in the talking pictures.[1]

When he began his second career, however, he was interested in neither talk nor pictures, but in music. In February 1919 he resolved that if he could put together enough capital, he would develop a new type of phonograph. "For the best of our phonographs today," he said,

> are merely crude & barbaric suggestions of the music they have essayed to record. And quite naturally so—for their *basic* principles—carving and cutting into a resisting solid; and then forcing and wiggling a stiff & crackling diaphragm—are fundamentally & hopelessly imperfect. No! *Light,* photography, selenium or photo-cell, the Audion (always the Audion!) and sounding board, or the reproducing bulb or flame—these are the elements which can capture and release music in all its beauty.[2]

De Forest was not the first to think of using light to record sound. The conventional phonograph, requiring the vibration of mechanical parts at high frequency, had always seemed crude when compared to the delicacy that might be achieved by a photographic system. As early as 1878, a scant year after Edison had perfected his mechanical talking machine, Professor E. W. Blake of Brown University made the first attempt to record sound with a beam of light on film. In the following forty years, more than two dozen inventors, including Alexander Graham Bell, worked on the problem.[3]

By September 1919 de Forest had joined that group. On 2 September he said that his second great goal in life (after inventing the triode) was to reproduce *real* music. "If I can succeed in this," he said, "the sheer joy of listening to such echoed music will be full reward for all my effort." In January 1920 he had his first success in converting voice from sound to light and back to sound. By September he was finding that each film record he made was better than the one before, and a month later he achieved his first reproduction of music that was recognizable as music.[4]

It was at about this time that he realized that his invention could be more than a phonograph, that it could be used to provide sound for motion pictures.[5] De Forest had been interested in movies for some time. In 1896, while he was a student at Yale, he witnessed a "Cinematograph" and pronounced it "wonderful." In 1912 he visited Edison's laboratories in New York and saw demonstrations of motion picture projectors and disc phonographs. The following year he tried to put image and sound together by recording sound on a steel wire that could be played back to accompany a motion picture. But in 1920 he realized that his new idea was even better. The steel wire, like an ordinary phonograph disc, had to be synchronized with film each time it was shown—a difficult process. But a *photographic* record could be attached to the film itself, as a "sound track," making synchronization automatic. Thus de Forest hoped his latest invention would not only improve the aural fidelity of words spoken by figures on the screen but also would make those words come out only when the figures' mouths were open. By November 1920 de Forest had decided to produce talking pictures rather than an improved phonograph. His invention, which hitherto he had called "Photophone," he now renamed "Phonofilm."[6]

In July 1921 he made his first experimental talking movie, a snippet of himself. In November 1922 he organized the De Forest Phonofilm Corp. to produce and market films and projection apparatus, and it was then that Theodore W. Case—another man destined for de Forest's rogues' gallery—entered the scene. As de Forest told the story in his autobiography, Case "came to see what I was doing, and became greatly interested. He learned quickly, and was soon a faithful imitator." In actuality, however, Case was no eager apprentice in the film industry but an experienced inventor who, with his assistant Earl I. Sponable, had already developed systems for recording and reproducing sound on film. As early as 1920 de Forest had found "very satisfactory" a photoelectric (Thalofide) cell that Case had invented; and by 1922 *all* the Phonofilm apparatus used that cell. Far from simply hiring Case as his assistant, de Forest leased the systems Case had already invented, then collaborated with Case and Sponable in producing further improvements. By the spring of 1923 de Forest was ready to show the results to the public. April 15 was opening night at the Rivoli Theater on Broadway, and de Forest presented clips of a serenade, a gavotte, and an Egyptian dance. The reviewer from the *Times* was disappointed to find that the music was "somewhat scratchy" and of no higher fidelity than the average phonograph's, but he was impressed by the perfect synchronization between picture and sound.[7]

"This Phonofilm work," said de Forest in July 1923, "is so immensely more interesting, artistic, & absorbing than Radio that I doubt if I can ever become really engrossed in those problems hereafter." As he worked on talking pictures, he found his affiliation with Radio Telephone & Telegraph an annoyance and a distraction. In 1921 he turned over the management of the company to two overseers. Two years later he sold his controlling interest in it for what he termed "a very large sum" (the *Times* reported it variously as $670,000 and about $1,000,000). Henceforth he would devote his life and fortune to the talkies.[8]

Between 1923 and 1927 de Forest made noteworthy films of notable people: Lillian Powell doing a bubble dance to the music of Brahms; De Wolf Hopper reciting "Casey at the Bat"; Eddie Cantor and George Jessel doing songs and monologues; Chauncey Depew reading "Recollections of Abraham Lincoln"; Doris Niles dancing; Charles Lindbergh being welcomed in Washington after his famous flight. Although he concentrated on "shorts"—musical numbers, monologues, and news clips—rather than photoplays, de Forest did produce a two-reel comic drama, *Love's Old Sweet Song* (with wife Mary in a singing role), in 1924. The following year he made his first talkie in color.[9]

In the summer of 1924 de Forest made a mark in the history of photojournalism by getting the presidential candidates of the three major parties on Phonofilm. As one might expect, he had difficulty with one of the nominees, "Silent Cal." President Coolidge agreed to the filming "very reluctantly," and when de Forest finally shot the footage, the Republican chief executive complained of the inconvenience and criticized the lighting.

Coolidge read a speech "in a lifeless voice," appearing "cross and put-out" all the while. When he finished, he "walked out of the picture (and out of our hearts!)."

The other candidates were more cooperative. When de Forest moved his equipment from the White House to the Senate Office Building, he found the Progressive Robert La Follette "all smiles and excitement; perfectly affable & *glad* to do whatever we asked of him." As a crowd of the curious gathered around, "Battle Bob" read a speech "with the greatest gusto"—so much, in fact, that the microphone malfunctioned. John W. Davis, the Democratic nominee, was also amiable. When filmed two weeks later, he impressed de Forest as being "by far the most pleasing personality of the three—a fine face, frank, clear, honest eyes—cordial & sincere."[10]

De Forest showed these newsreels at thirty theaters during the campaign. In September the New York *Times* reviewed the films, saying that the remarkable thing about them was that in spite of the "hollow, horn-like reproduction," there was no doubt about the individuality of the speakers. People who knew the candidates would have no trouble recognizing their distinctive voices. La Follette's was louder than the others', said the *Times,* "and this fact was more apparent when he stressed a thought with a movement of his fist."[11]

Coolidge, La Follette, Lindbergh—some of America's most celebrated men appeared on Phonofilm. De Forest took pleasure in recording for posterity their looks and words. To him it seemed that the cinematographer should be as much a historian as an artist. One of the principal functions of Phonofilm, he told a Rotary luncheon group, would be to record for posterity the voices of immortal men. Regretting that Abraham Lincoln and Theodore Roosevelt had died before talking pictures were invented, de Forest said that Phonofilm would provide vivid and lasting impressions of future heroes. "That these great moments in the lives of great men shall not be forever lost to our descendants," he told the Society of Motion Picture Engineers, "is one of the debts which those who come after us shall owe to the film which records both the voice and the visage of the nation's leaders." Doubtless, de Forest was thinking of Longfellow's lines:

> Lives of great men all remind us
> We can make our lives sublime. . . .

Thanks to Phonofilm, future Americans could be reminded of great men of the past and could thereby be inspired to make their own lives sublime. Thus, de Forest hoped to immortalize men like Lindbergh by leaving film prints on the sands of time—and, in so doing, to immortalize himself as a benefactor of mankind.[12]

Meanwhile, though, de Forest was forsaking the laboratory research upon which his place in history would rest. After the spring of 1923 he left most experimentation to his collaborators, Case and Sponable, devoting his own time to learning to take pictures and promoting Phonofilm sales. Case and Sponable, he later admitted, designed a sound camera that was "distinctly better than any predecessor"; and de Forest used adaptations of that camera to make Phonofilms. According to motion picture historian Kenneth Macgowan, de Forest took charge of production and exhibition while Case and Sponable made "the greatest technical advances."[13]

Unfortunately, de Forest the producer lacked the imagination of de Forest the inventor. Film historian Miles Kreuger says that de Forest cared little about full-length features and contented himself with "shorts." His inability to take films seriously as works of art made him neglect even to copyright any of them—an astounding lapse in a man so often embroiled in lawsuits over patents. Moreover, he was so indifferent to film as a *visual* art that he never even used a second camera. Lee de Forest was no D. W. Griffith.[14]

As a promoter, de Forest had little success. To his dismay, Hollywood was no more eager for sound film in 1925 than New York had been for radio in 1900. Individual theaters might purchase Phonofilm projection apparatus and show de Forest's pictures, but nationwide chains held back. For them, silent movies were profitable enough. In 1922 de Forest tried to sell the Phonofilm system to William Fox but was not even granted an interview. Two years later, when Fox heard that Phonofilm equipment had been installed in six of his theaters, he ordered it removed. Such conservatism reinforced de Forest's old conviction that big capitalists lacked imagination.[15]

Although no major motion picture studio or theater chain would switch on to sound, some small entrepreneurs were more daring. By the fall of 1924 more than thirty theaters had been equipped for Phonofilm, and fifty more were awaiting installation. "Taking it all in all," de Forest told a meeting of the Society of Motion Picture Engineers, "we feel very much encouraged by the result of the past years' efforts and believe that after five years of strenuous and often discouraging labor we are about to meet our reward."[16]

In private, however, de Forest was worried. In the summer of 1924 he noted in his journal that he was almost out of money to continue production. In 1925, having spent $200,000 of his own funds, he resorted to selling stock to the public, an action which had brought him many legal problems in the past. Thanks to an aggressive sales campaign, the treasury soon began to fill up. Unfortunately, the sales campaign was a little *too* aggressive, irritating (among others) the president of the United States and the attorney general of the State of New York. When making their pitch, de Forest's agents showed the Phonofilm newsreel of Calvin Coolidge and made liberal use of his name. When the president heard of this, he protested that the film had been made with the understanding that it would be shown only during the political campaign. De Forest replied that he had made no such agreement. Coolidge ordered an investigation by the Justice Department.[17]

As it happened, however, the federal government proved less bothersome than the state. In May 1925, the same month that Coolidge tried to get out of the picture, the New York Bureau for Prevention of Frauds began looking into De Forest Phonofilm. Deciding that the company was financially unsound, the state forbade the sale of stock. Newspapers joined in the attack, and the exasperated De Forest began to suspect that rival moviemakers were behind this "attempt to wreck my last & greatest enterprise." Firing his old attorneys, he retained Arthur Garfield Hays (who a few months later would head for Dayton, Tennessee, to help defend John Scopes from William Jennings Bryan and the fundamentalists). But it was already too late. "The large financial assistance which the public was affording Phonofilm," de Forest lamented, "has been quite stopped & the day of freedom from worry, which I had at last forseen, is yet further postponed."[18]

As if government investigations did not weaken the company enough, De Forest Phonofilm was riven by infighting. In September 1925 Theodore Case ended his collaboration with de Forest and withdrew the license of De Forest Phonofilm to use his inventions. Historian Miles Kreuger blames Case's departure on his disgust with de Forest's lack of "artistic vision," but it may have been due also to professional rivalry between the inventors. In 1924 Case complained of how some Phonofilms' opening credits failed to include "in large title letters, 'Taken by Case Studios.'" The following year he insisted on a new contract; but de Forest thought that he could replace the Case apparatus with others and that Case's demands were exorbitant. Hence the breakup. Nor was

Case the only one in the firm with whom de Forest was having problems. When a road show touring New England lost four thousand dollars, de Forest berated the advisers who had persuaded him to sponsor it. By the end of 1925 he believed that his commercial associates were "a gang of enemies . . . who while I trusted them showed again & again their fixed determination to batten off my efforts & brains—to strip me, dominate me, & grow fat off my genius, my effort." In the movies as in radio, he felt he was being robbed by false friends and deprived of his just deserts.[19]

But he was not without hope. In March 1926 he said that the corner was nearly turned, that (mixing the metaphors) Phonofilm was nearly over the top. "It now represents 6 years of my life & *all* my fortune," he observed. "It *must* win out." Nineteen twenty-six would be a critical year.[20]

During the years that de Forest sank his radio earnings into Phonofilm, he began to think about economy. "My household bills are terrific," he noted in August 1920; in November he calculated that his personal expenses were more than $1,500 a month. In an attempt to save money, he moved his factory and household to Berlin in October 1921, figuring that American dollars would stretch far in inflation-ridden Germany. The move was a mistake. On the professional side, photographic equipment and skilled workers were hard to find, so production lagged. On the personal side, de Forest was depressed by the scarcity of English-speaking companions, by the severity of the climate, and by the political unrest. His wife, Mary, had an additional disappointment. She had gone to Europe with the hope of joining an opera company. Finding no such opportunity, she sought solace with her old friend the bottle, which did not add to her husband's contentment. In September 1922 the inventor returned to New York. His wife and child, however, moved into a chateau on the Riviera, where they remained until the following June.[21]

The de Forests argued often about money. "She *will not* scrounge—she *will not* help," complained the man of the house in October 1920. Whenever he gave her a hundred dollars, he said, she would spend it within a week. Time and again he had to redeem her rings from pawn. If he exhorted her to save money by taking the train when she went downtown, she would angrily insist on being driven by auto. But although he berated Mary for improvidence, de Forest himself did not pinch pennies unduly hard. His household included "four in help"—a chauffeur, a cook, a housemaid, and a nursemaid; in 1923 he enlarged and remodeled his mansion, Riverlure. Nine months before imploring Mary to ride the train, he bought a Cadillac. Eight months *after* the scolding, he bought a Rolls Royce. He toured Europe in a Pierce Arrow, and when he returned to America, he sailed first class. While de Forest accused Mary of extravagance, she tongue-lashed him for recklessness. Noting that his expenses greatly exceeded his income, de Forest had tried to rectify the situation by speculating on the stock market. Unfortunately, his investments proved unsound and he was "well cursed (by self & wife!) for my folly."[22]

Besides excessive drinking and excessive spending, there was another important source of discord—excessive work. Still among the "Driven Ones," the inventor could not spare time for his family. While he was in California in 1919 on his second honeymoon, his pleasure was dampened by the thought that his laboratory was far away and that time was flying. Over a year later, regretting that he could not fully enjoy the company of his daughter Eleanor, he said that his "mind cells are poisoned with this cursed zeal for work, to solve my problem—& grasp the reward." Always thinking of his work and his "reward," de Forest was damned even in the midst of paradise. On a hike in 1923 he enjoyed the scenery until he realized "that all this seductive loveliness is a glorious Delilah, robbing me of my strength, to deliver me to the Phillistines, a slave to beauty, *but alas,* an idle, *workless* slave!" De Forest's work often took him away from home—to Baltimore, Chicago, Washington, Europe. Moreover, even when he was in New York, he forsook the home for the laboratory. One Thanksgiving Day an infuriated Mary, having prepared an elaborate dinner, had to storm downtown and drag her husband away from an experiment.[23]

The year 1924 brought a new strain on the marriage: Mary was pregnant again. Although Eleanor's birth in 1919 had helped bring the couple back together, this second pregnancy pushed them further apart. De Forest was delighted with the prospect of another child—he talked with Eleanor about the "little brother" who would soon join her—but Mary was not so pleased. Remembering the pain of her previous childbirth, she told her husband that she did not want another baby and that if he wanted one so badly, he should bear it himself. Mary's dread was warranted. She underwent long nights of frequenting vomiting and severe back pain before finally giving birth on 1 December 1924. As before, the father felt intense surprise and chagrin when the child proved to be a girl. But as before, both he and Mary came to adore the "cunning little weazened red face" of the stranger, whom they named Marilyn. "No mother," said de Forest approvingly, "could be fonder than is Mary of both her little girls . . . What a mother's heart is here!"[24]

De Forest had a high regard for mother's hearts: ever since he had left home, his relationship with his own mother had been perfectly amicable. She still begged him to bear his honors meekly and to seek Christ, but she also took pride in her son's honors and thanked him heartily for the presents he sent her. Having followed de Forest to Palo Alto in 1912, she remained there after he returned east in 1913. In subsequent years he wrote to her almost every Sunday. De Forest also was on good terms with his sister, Mary, who in 1901 had married a minister, Philip Ralph. She, too, received letters and gifts, and the Ralphs named the second of their sons Philip Lee (the first was Henry).[25]

Rather surprising, perhaps, was the cordiality between de Forest and his former antagonist, his brother Charles. Leaving Yale Law School in 1904 to make a career in business, Charles invested in a number of speculative stocks, among them American De Forest Wireless Telegraph. Finding himself broke in 1913, Charles started a new career: social service. He worked for the Red Cross, the New York State Charities Aid Association, and the National Tuberculosis Association. In 1916 he founded the Children's Modern Health Crusade, a campaign to encourage schoolchildren to wash their hands and brush their teeth, to drink water but not coffee, to play outdoors, and to keep neat and cheerful. From 1928 to 1947 he was executive vice president of the American Provident Society, an organization teaching thrift. During the Great Depression he wrote pamphlets with titles like "How Old Am I Financially?" (1930) and "My Savings Timetable" (1937). Like his father and brother, Charles sought to improve mankind.[26]

The two brothers got along better in middle age than in youth. In 1926 Lee admired the courageous spirit of his "stalwart brother," whose wife was dying of heart disease. In 1931, when Charles was working for the Provident Society, Lee told him that he was right to preach saving. Lee gave money to his brother during hard times, and for that Charles was "eternally thankful." Four years after Charles's death in 1947, Lee made a contribution in his memory to the Yale Alumni Fund.[27]

Since 1916, when he had banged the drums for preparedness,

de Forest had seen himself as a spokesman for the public interest, and in the twenties he took it upon himself to raise the cultural level of the masses. At a Rotary Club luncheon in March 1924 he began a campaign for better radio programming that was to last a quarter century. Although eight years earlier he had broadcast sales pitches for de Forest radio receivers, he now declared that ads should be banned from the airwaves. The broadcasters' loss in revenues from advertisers, he said, would be more than offset by the increase in sales of receiving sets which would occur once listeners knew they would not be subjected to huckstering (in those days, stations often were owned by radio manufacturers). The important thing was that with advertising gone, broadcasters could devote themselves entirely to good music and instructive programs. Interviewed by *Success Magazine*, de Forest said that his ruling ambition in developing radio had been to see it bring "the very best in entertainment, education, information" into every home.[28]

Not only radio, but also sound film, was to raise aesthetic and intellectual standards. In 1924, after recording a musical accompaniment to James Cruze's spectacular film *The Covered Wagon*, de Forest believed he had "shown the way for educating the masses, insiduously, unaware of the uplift (and therefore the more effective) to better & more worthy music." Two years later he suggested that Phonofilm, by providing good reproduction of good music, would "in time elevate the present undeniably low level of taste and intelligence of the average motion picture audience." Nor would the uplift be solely musical. Poetry readings recorded on Phonofilm would instill in theatergoers a love of verse, and historical movies would invigorate patriotism. As a progressive and an evolutionist, de Forest believed that his inventions would spur the advance of civilization. In middle age as in youth, he foresaw technology creating utopia.[29]

Meanwhile, the De Forest Phonofilm Co. was lurching toward insolvency. By 1926 de Forest's personal fortune had been nearly exhausted, and the company's revenues were low. Then, in July of that year, the inventor received "a shock, like a blow." Posters in New York were advertising Warner Brothers' "Vitaphone," the first system for talking pictures to be used by a major studio. Engineered by Western Electric and consisting essentially of a phonograph disc synchronized with a film, Vitaphone was less innovative and in the long run less practical than the sound-on-film system of de Forest. Nevertheless, it worked well enough to bring crowds to see John Barrymore in *Don Juan* (1926) and Al Jolson in *The Jazz Singer* (1927).[30]

Although at first dismayed by Vitaphone's success, de Forest soon cheered up, believing it would waken Warner Brothers' rivals to the possibilities of Phonofilm. In October 1926 his hopes seemed justified. William Fox, who had spurned two previous offers, paid $100,000 for the option to buy controlling interest in De Forest Phonofilm one month later for $2,400,000. "So it appears," rejoiced the inventor, "that I'm about to cash in handsomely."[31]

But once again appearances deceived. Fox's acquisition of the option had been merely a precaution, for he had already purchased rights to a talking-picture system from de Forest's recent associate, Theodore Case. In the fall of 1925, Case had ended his informal collaboration with de Forest and had continued research independently; in July 1926—just as Vitaphone appeared—he had sold his system to Fox. Although Case had been working on talkies since 1911, had made several inventions which de Forest used in Phonofilm, and had surpassed de Forest in research between 1923 and 1925, Fox at first was not certain that Case had complete legal title to his system. Therefore, in October 1926, three months after buying the Case system, Fox took out the option on Phonofilm. When the time came to complete the transaction, however, the magnate decided that Case's title was secure and therefore allowed the option to lapse. Fox sacrificed a hundred thousand dollars but saved himself—and cost De Forest— over two million. The newly formed Fox-Case Corp. called its sound-on-film system Movietone and by January 1927 produced its first motion picture.[32]

Infuriated by Fox's "kyke-like . . . devilish machinations," de Forest pressed lawsuits alleging that Case's system infringed on patents held by De Forest Phonofilm. Eventually de Forest received an out-of-court settlement of sixty thousand dollars, far from enough to satisfy someone who had expected to be made a millionaire. In 1928 two South African capitalists invested in De Forest Phonofilm and reorganized it as General Talking Pictures Corp., with de Forest reduced to the role of vice president. After consuming a decade of de Forest's life and nearly all his wealth, the talking-picture dream faded out.[33]

On the private level as well as the professional, 1926 began with high hopes and ended in disaster. In the previous years de Forest's marriage had been troubled. Sometimes Mary had been "sweet and deeply loving & therefore deeply lovable"; at other times, she had drunk herself senseless, and de Forest "would flee as from a pestilence—this sickening curse of my life." In 1926 matters were brought to a head by Mary's third pregnancy.[34]

"Perhaps even now," wrote de Forest in November 1925, "the new life that begins may yet prove the goals of all my years-old hopes—my fond desires, even when in college, of myself tasting the priceless joy of having a son's companionship—the pride of having a son at Yale!" As the months of gestation passed, de Forest happily plotted the future, planning to name his son Lee Jr. and to enroll him in Yale's class of '48. Perhaps, he figured, the boy would even become an inventor, carrying on his father's work as well as his name (shades of Henry de Forest!).[35]

While de Forest dreamed, his wife endured. From November on, Mary suffered continual nausea and spent most of each day in bed; by early April she was wan and thin. Medical specialists could not explain her malady. Growing frailer day by day, she kept up her spirits with liquor. On 15 April Mary gave birth to an eight-and-a-half pound boy. Two days later the child died. "It is a cruel blow to me," wrote the father in his journal, "after waiting & vainly hoping all these years for a Son!"

> I had for years come to a gradual abandonment of my youthful dreams of an heir, a *Companion* in my Son. These dead hopes had only recently become reawakened. So now I can steel my heart to bury them once more, in the little casket in Greenwood.

Doctors told him that the boy had died from a diseased thyroid, and de Forest found vent for his disappointment and grief. "Unquestionably," he said, the baby's glandular disorder was due to "the poisonous alcohol which his mother had so persistently taken." But if de Forest was in a mood to scold, his wife was in no condition to listen. After the birth Mary's health declined still further. The night following the delivery she became hysterical. So weakened was she that de Forest waited a week before telling her of the child's death, fearing that the news might be too much for her. When finally informed, she "wept bitterly" and could not sleep. A week later she still looked "sad and wan as a bereaved Madonna"; and on Mother's Day, de Forest reported that Mary had been spending the springtime in bed, crying.[36]

On 13 May the convalescent mother, with daughters Eleanor and Marilyn in tow, boarded a liner sailing for Europe. De Forest, staying behind, hoped that the cruise would "do for her what doctors & nurses . . . have failed to do." But the trip did not have the therapeutic results he had envisioned. Once free, Mary chose not to return to her husband, and in 1929 they were divorced.[37]

For de Forest the second half of the Roaring Twenties was a time of gloom. His radio work had ended, and his movie work had failed. Anna de Forest died in June 1927 at the age of seventy-nine, bringing her son further grief. In August of that year, de Forest moaned that all his disappointments were bringing him near despair. After Mary Mayo had left him, he found solace in the company of a divorcée named Henrietta Tilghman O'Kelly, for whose apartment he paid the rent; but that affair turned sour, and de Forest resented having to give money to that "viperess." By April 1929 the inventor, who had never been particularly fond of New York, began thinking of escape. "I long to look at flowers," he said, "instead of foreigners." By the summer of 1930 de Forest had one more reason to flee—another woman. One Miriam, from Great Neck, Long Island, was writing to him, saying, "I am praying to Venus, Eros, Kama, that the fire which sprang up between us will not turn to ashes and that my devotion to you and my confidence in you is not misplaced." Within days, de Forest moved to California.[38]

6

At Last, at Last: 1931

When Lee de Forest headed west in 1930, he left behind the reminders of a lifetime of defeats: a squandered fortune, three wrecked marriages, a dead son. He could never regain what he had lost. Time does not heal; it buries. Still, de Forest could hope for something better. Did not Longfellow urge him to act in the living present instead of brooding over the dead past? And did not Tennyson assure him that good would fall at last to all? And where but California, the Golden State, would winter soonest change to spring? Dreams might come true after all.

De Forest returned to California in August 1930. On Saturday the thirtieth, he was invited to a beach party in Santa Monica at the home of motion picture actress Bebe Daniels, a distant cousin of his. While relaxing in the surf, de Forest conversed with one of the other guests, a woman named Marie Mosquini. Later, at the house, Daniels attempted to provide the two with a formal introduction, but de Forest would not allow it. In future years, he said, he wanted to be able to say that he and Marie had been introduced by no one but the sea. De Forest was never one to shilly-shally. On 3 October, less than five weeks after meeting, he and Marie were married in Mexico. For him it was the fourth marriage, for her the second, and for both the last.[1]

Marie already had had an eventful life. The child of well-to-do immigrants (her father was from Italy, her mother from France), she had been sent to a convent to learn English. Leaving school at age thirteen, she worked as a stenographer before being "discovered" by movie producer Hal Roach. Marie played in numerous short comedies with Harold Lloyd, then was Will Rogers' leading lady in two dozen more. At the time of her marriage she was in the midst of filming her first talking picture.[2]

For a person who had tasted fame, Marie showed little ambition. "I wasn't interested in being a star," she recalled years later. "All I wanted to do was to get married." While working in show

"At last, at last," 1931. De Forest, film star Bebe Daniels (a colonel in the Army Air Corps), and Marie Mosquini, recently retired from movies and now de Forest's fourth and final wife. Photo courtesy of Perham Foundation.

business, she told her mother that all she desired was to act in one big dramatic picture, then marry a great man. After marrying Lee de Forest, she gave up her career. "Nothing, nothing," she said, "ever came before my husband." Beautiful, talented, and selfless, Marie was all that de Forest had hoped for. He called her "Mi Mijita," which she translated from the Spanish as "My dear. My loved one. My own. My everything." In June 1931 he told his brother how happy he was to be in California with a California girl. "Seems now," he said, "that at last, at last after all those cursed, *joyless* years, I have really begun to live!"[3]

When he moved west in 1930, de Forest did so for professional reasons as well as personal. He wanted to continue working on talking pictures, and Hollywood was the logical place for that. In addition he planned to do research on ultra–high-frequency radio transmission, and he believed that static interference was less troublesome in California than in New York. During the next three decades, the inventor worked on these problems and many more. Although he made no inventions comparable in importance to the Audion, he continued to show ingenuity, ambition, and determination.[4]

Perhaps the one concern that occupied him most was television. Having brought sound to motion pictures, he now wanted to send pictures via the radio waves along with sound. When he moved to California, it was in the midst of television's first flowering—a fatally premature one, as it turned out. In 1925 C. Francis Jenkins had demonstrated a workable TV system using mechanical scanning devices (as opposed to purely electronic ones) and producing "low-definition" (i.e., fuzzy) images, and it wasn't long before Lee de Forest got into the picture. De Forest Radio Co. and de Forest himself collaborated with the Jenkins Television Corp. in the New York City area. James W. Garside, the president of De Forest Radio, also became the first president of Jenkins TV in 1928. By 1930 the Jenkins TV station was broadcasting pictures that were synchronized with an audio portion broadcast from De Forest Radio's station in Passaic, New Jersey. The standard program included a clip of de Forest expounding on the future of television. Thus as early as 1930, Lee de Forest was a TV personality.[5]

When he moved to Los Angeles later that year, he continued to follow Jenkins's lead by approaching television in terms of mechanical engineering, using a rotating drum for a scanning device—a system he called "tele-film." Like other users of mechanical systems, however, de Forest was unable to produce sharp pictures—a crucial flaw. As historian Joseph Udelson has shown, the engineering limitations of early television caused the boom to collapse by 1933. It was in that year, as the Great Depression dried up investors' capital, that Lee de Forest abandoned his "tele-film" for lack of funds. Perhaps it was just as well. While de Forest continued to use a mechanical scanning device, V. K. Zworykin of RCA and the independent inventor Philo Farnsworth separately sought an electronic solution. As they developed the cathode-ray tube, de Forest said that it was not the radical innovation needed. As it turned out, however, he was wrong: the cathode-ray system produced high-definition images, sparked a new television boom after World War II, and continues to serve in today's TV. In 1946 de Forest resumed his tinkering with television, this time trying to bring color to the tube. As before, he tried to devise a mechanical scanning system. RCA acquired the rights to his system but abandoned it in favor of an electronic one.[6]

For television, as for radio earlier, de Forest had high hopes. In a book published in 1942 he predicted that TV would be a profitable industry within three years. Manufacturers would sell sets not only for viewing at home but also for such purposes as factory supervision, traffic control, and aviation. Broadcasters would make money through sale of advertising (the ads, of course, would be "inoffensive"). In addition to producing profits, television would raise the level of civilization. It would educate viewers, and it would strengthen families by inducing children to stay at home. There was little chance, de Forest believed, that television programs would be as "moronic" as radio programs; for although audiences might be willing to *hear* banal performances, they would never tolerate *seeing* them. "In television," predicted the prophet of progress through technology, "the criterions of merit will inevitably be placed high."[7]

Television was de Forest's main research interest after 1930, but it was hardly his only one. Beginning in 1934, de Forest studied diathermy, the heating of human tissue by passing electric currents through it. Such research in medical technology appealed to him strongly, for it was "highly interesting, humanitarian, presumably profitable." Until 1947 he designed and manufactured diathermy machines. During World War II de Forest worked on airplane speed, course, and altitude indicators, and a self-directing bomb. In the 1950s, returning to a project from his Yale days, he attempted to convert solar energy to electric current. All told, he received more than three hundred patents, the last of which (on an automatic telephone dialing device) was granted when he was eighty-four years old. As Rupert Maclaurin says, he was "perhaps the most imaginative inventor in the history of the radio enterprise."[8]

But imagination is not invention: the machines de Forest built in his later years simply did not work. When his self-directing bomb was tested, it veered off course and nearly landed on top of de Forest and an army general who was there to observe. At about the same time, de Forest tried to develop a telephone answering machine; but as Tom Lewis has pointed out, it was a device worthy of Rube Goldberg. A motor was to raise a hook, which would lift a telephone receiver and swing it to face a tape recorder; after a message was recorded, the motor could go into reverse and swing the receiver back into place. This answering machine resembled de Forest's television in relying on mechanical rather than electronic engineering. "Curiously," says Lewis, "the first person to harness the electron in a significant way relied on machinery to accomplish the tasks an electrical circuit could perform far more efficiently."[9]

From a fiscal standpoint, too, de Forest's last three decades were not very productive: no subsequent invention would prove as profitable as the triode. In 1936 he declared bankruptcy, with liabilities of $104,000 and assets of $390. Never again would he enjoy the security and independence provided by a personal fortune. He was employed by American Television Laboratories of Chicago in the late forties (spending winters in California and the rest of the time in Chicago) and by United Engineering Laboratories of Los Angeles in the fifties. In 1950 he organized the Lee de Forest Foundation, a tax shelter which in three years dispensed six thousand dollars to charities (about half of that went to Talladega College) and thirty-one thousand to its director, Lee de Forest. In his last years he received fifteen thousand dollars annually from Bell Labs in return for consulting. The house in which he lived was the property of his wife.[10]

The ever-impecunious inventor sought ways to supplement his salary. In 1944 he was declared eligible for a veteran's pension, based on his service in the Spanish-American War; in 1956 he applied for Social Security. In 1952, when Sylvania asked him to pose for a publicity photo showing him holding the billionth vacuum tube manufactured by the company, he demanded and got a thousand-dollar fee. Seven years later, after being interviewed by CBS, he suggested that the network compensate him for his time.[11]

CBS may have been surprised by the request, for de Forest had never been camera shy. Since he had first achieved fame, he had enjoyed playing the role of the public man. Although he never devoted much time to any political organization, he sought to effect reform through the individualistic means of speeches, magazine and newspaper articles, and letters.

De Forest's main worry continued to be the low quality of radio programming. In 1946, when the National Association of Broadcasters met in Chicago, he sent them a letter that made headlines. Calling himself the father of radio broadcasting, he mourned his "child" by deploring the pop music, advertising, and murder mysteries that dominated the ether. Broadcasting, he said, was conceived as a potent instrument for spreading fine culture and uplifting the mass intelligence. But radio stations had debased the child by sending him onto the streets in "rags and ragtime, tatters of jive and boogie woogie, to collect money from all and sundry." In contrast, the child's English brother, raised under government sponsorship, had been taught that its mission was to elevate and not to degrade. De Forest hoped that someday American radio too would appeal "to the higher intelligence." When he published his autobiography in 1950, de Forest called on state legislatures to subsidize "good music" stations. "To this extent," he said, "I am a socialist." Through his critique of radio, the "father" won a measure of fame. In 1955 magazine columnist Bennett Cerf reported that the inventor was disappointed with his brainchild and was calling it "de Forest's prime evil."[12]

Next to radio spots and boogie woogie, it was communism that drew de Forest's most vociferous attacks. In the 1930s he worried privately about the "half-baked, Communistic theories of Upton Sinclair" and warned his reform-minded former mother-in-law not to be taken in by the communists. It was not till the fifties, however, that the Red Menace became a major concern for him. In November 1952 he wrote to the U.S. Parole Board to protest against any possible future release of the "arch traitor" Alger Hiss; in the same month he wrote to Hiss's nemesis, newly elected Vice President Richard Nixon, urging him to "prosecute with renewed vigor your valiant fight to put out Communism from every branch of our government." In December 1953 he told Senator Joseph McCarthy that he was "unable to praise you sufficiently," and he warned President Eisenhower that the Wisconsin senator deserved praise, not censure, for his patriotism. That same month de Forest canceled his subscription to the *Nation,* averring that the magazine was "lousy with Treason, crawling with Communism." In October 1954 he denounced the *Yale Scientific Magazine* for printing an "Anti-anti-Communism diatribe" and implored the

"Achesonian scoffers" to cease typing as "paranoids" those brave souls who exposed "the vermin gnawing at our Nation's entrails."[13]

Although anticommunism was a crusade he entered only in the 1950s, the rhetoric had long been his. The idea of subversion, of corruption within, had troubled him for decades. In 1930 he had spoken of an "insidious influence" that would "sap the life blood"—but at that time he had been talking about radio advertising and its effect on the public. The following year he had written to the Sons of the Revolution about "Borers from within"—but in that instance he had meant "the venal politician, the secret or avowed agent of great monied interests, the grafter in office, and the criminal." In the 1950s he still believed that America was overrun by subversives, but now they were communists instead of racketeers, financiers, or sponsors of radio commercials.[14]

De Forest's anticommunism jibed with the rest of his politics: conservative and Republican. It is true that in 1932, when the country was in the Great Depression and de Forest himself was nearly destitute, he was sufficiently desperate to vote for Franklin Roosevelt. On the night of the first Fireside Chat, de Forest enjoyed the President's "sensible reassuring words." But the Depression ended, and so did de Forest's fling with the liberal Democrat. Inconvenienced by a transit strike in 1946, he blamed the "evil might of the badly-led labor unions" on America's "first *Fascist* President, F.D.R." In 1949 he sent letters to all members of Congress, urging them to vote against socialized medicine, federally subsidized housing, and an excess-profits tax. He considered Harry Truman and "Red butchers" equally responsible for the death of American troops in Korea, and in 1951 he told Douglas MacArthur that the nation needed the general as president. As it turned out, however, one old soldier was as good as another. In January 1953 de Forest told how happy he was that the United States was to be governed by "so rare a gift of God to man as is Prest. Eisenhouser and the wise, experienced buisness men he has selected to aid him." In that same year he wrote to Senator Pat McCarran, expressing continued support for immigration restriction, and to Eisenhower himself, suggesting tax reductions. In 1957 de Forest served as chairman of the Free Enterprise Foundation.[15]

In the 1950s the inventor became an irrepressible letter writer, and the recipients of his missives were not always statesmen and generals. Again and again he wrote to officials of Los Angeles, complaining of spilled gravel on streets, of broken pavements, of faulty mail and telegram delivery, of erroneous billings, of defective products. Partly, it seems, he undertook complaint in the public interest, as a self-appointed ombudsman. In 1953, for instance, he wrote to the owner of the building that housed his laboratory, protesting against the forced retirement of a sixty-five-year-old handyman (de Forest was eighty at the time). That same year, after watching a television performance of Bob Hope before an audience of sailors, the inventor fired off a telegram which informed the comedian that his show was "a disgrace to you and an insult to our Navy." When Hope asked what sin he had committed, de Forest replied that one of Hope's routines had homosexual overtones that were "suggestive of evil to the young navy sailors." Having corrected the corrupter of youth, de Forest wanted to make certain that he himself never shared in the crime. In August 1953, when he was thinking of appearing on the Ed Sullivan television show, he inquired whether the program was "high class and dignified." He did not want to be surrounded, he said, "by more or less nude chorus girls."[16]

De Forest, son of a preacher, had long perceived a decline in public decency. Since the Great War, he wrote in 1935, there had been "a definite deterioration of general moral tone" all over the world. Although the decay was global, it seemed especially advanced in the United States. The Olympics of 1932, held in Los Angeles, vividly demonstrated to de Forest the rottenness at the nation's core. Watching the ceremonies, he was impressed by the parade of proud and dignified foreign athletes but ashamed of the sloppy Americans. The Yanks were so lacking in discipline and respect, he reported, that they sat or lay down during the dedication address, benediction, and sacred hymn. This excessive casualness, he said, was "the natural result of American civilization of today—her lax home-training, her diet of Hollywood's sex & crime-films, universal auto-ownership with resultant loss of knowledge of how to use the limbs." Five months later, on New Year's Eve, he was treated once again to a spectacle of degeneration. A California radio station broadcast live coverage of celebrations as the midnight hour moved westward across the country, and de Forest listened in to assess the state of the union. At 9 o'clock, Pacific Standard Time, he heard "the loud, zoo-like yelling and shrilling from the gin-stimulated jews and gunmen staggering about Times Square." Later he found that Chicago's "morons and inflamed youth differed in no observable quality or degree of insanity from the bacteriological cultures collected an hour earlier in the East." America, de Forest discovered, was in the hands of "mad and epileptic mobs."[17]

The country was in terrible shape, aswarm with maniacal revelers, lazy athletes, lewd comedians, communist subversives, and unscrupulous radio advertisers. Nevertheless, de Forest did not despair. In the same 1935 letter in which he reported the world-wide deterioration of moral tone, he also asserted his faith that education was gradually filtering from the school to the home and would eventually transform "the child-like brain of Man." "Despite all the appalling depressions in the graph of man's progress from the slime," he said, "its general trend is inescapably upward." De Forest never forgot the dream of progress that he had experienced as a college undergraduate. Despite his political conservatism, he still thought of himself as a progressive. Paradise was still in reach, and it still would be attained through advances in technology.[18]

The first step was an end to war, and this would be achieved partly through the invention of increasingly lethal weapons. De Forest had first stated this argument in 1895 in his *Yale Scientific Monthly* article, "Progress in Aerial Navigation." The airplane, he had said, would make warfare so destructive that no nation would dare engage in it. Four decades later in a follow-up article, "Progress in Aerial Navigation—1934," he acknowledged that the Great War might seem to have been "a ghastly refutation" of his 1895 prediction. Nevertheless, his faith remained unshaken.

> One may assuredly hope [he said] that one more such lesson in devastation . . . may teach even the stupid criminals who decree war that it *cannot be.*
> And surely the airplane and Zeppelin have done more to hasten that final millenium than all the peace pacts ever penned.

Air forces and Luftwaffes, he prophesied in 1934, would keep war from happening ever again.[19]

De Forest's sanguine prophecy may have been naive, but it was not abnormal. Even before the airplane existed, people imagined it the antidote to war. In 1864 Victor Hugo foresaw that flying machines would rid the world of "the whole business of war, exploitation, and subjugation." In 1905, a year and a half after the Wright brothers' first flight at Kitty Hawk, their adviser Octave Chanute predicted that their invention would "deter embroilments." After World War I, gyroscope inventor Elmo Sperry prophesied that aerial torpedoes would make war "so extremely hazardous and expensive that no nation will dare go into it," while the widely admired military strategists Giulio Douhet and Basil Liddell Hart predicted that air power would make a future war briefer and less bloody than the previous one.[20]

As historian Michael Sherry has pointed out, this belief that swords were preparing the ground for plowshares stemmed from the modern era's faith in science and reason. If people were rational, they could see that war in an age of air power was suicidal; therefore, they would not go to war. Lee de Forest shared this confidence in human reason and believed that inventions, even ones as sinister as long-range bombers, would bring on the millenium.[21]

But air power was not the only contribution that technology would make to peace. Radio and television, he believed, would also be important, for improved communication would make conflict less likely. Television, he said at the height of the Cold War, was the *"ultimate instrument."* International broadcasting would diminish fear and suspicion by spreading the truth and by uniting all races and nationalities in common emotional and intellectual experiences. Radio also would help. First through music, then through the dissemination of a universal language, it would bring a sense of neighborliness to all the world. Like TV, radio would expose falsehoods and eradicate suspicion, thus making possible "an *International understanding based on Truth.*" To further this "interchange of ideas," he gave an unqualified endorsement to Radio Free Europe.[22]

Besides putting an end to war, engineering would enrich the lives of all the world's citizens. Radio, de Forest believed, was beginning to do so already. Despite its shortcomings, it brought "beauty and culture and truth into the human heart," thus proving "one of the greatest comforts and blessings which mankind has ever found." Beneficent as it already was, it would be even better in the future. In 1930 de Forest predicted that by 1980 receiving sets would be more efficient; more important, commercials would be banned at last. Other inventions also would promote the general welfare. Television would bring motion pictures into the home, and electric automobiles would make travel noiseless and clean. The discovery of new sources of energy (including atomic power), he said in 1923, would make the good life available to all. In 1931 the visionary engineer told a conclave of his fellows that "since the dawn of history the world owes far more to its Inventors than to any other class of men." In maturity as in youth, he believed that engineers would build the stairway to heaven.[23]

Moreover, the look of paradise had not changed much since 1895. It still would be a modernistic reproduction of small-town America. In 1930, when a reporter asked de Forest what New York would be like fifty years hence, the inventor predicted that it would not be so big. Improved communication and transportation would decentralize the city, with the rich, the poor, and the prolific streaming out of Manhattan. (The poor, he said, would settle in garden villas in Queens, Nassau, and New Jersey; he did not speculate on the fate of the rich and of middle-class people with large families.) All who would remain on the island would be artists, executives, professionals, and others who had few children. With population diffused, rebuilding could commence. Skyscrapers would be leveled, and handsome, healthful residences put in their place. New Yorkers would be much happier in 1980 than in 1930. "Why not?" asked de Forest. "Won't there be fewer of us?"[24]

As de Forest placed his hopes for the future on a man-made utopia, he continued to disparage the "ancient myths." In 1932 the Los Angeles *Times* carried a symposium called "What Is Heaven . . . and Where?" Representatives of various religions and philosophies provided short answers, with de Forest speaking for the agnostics. Maintaining that consciousness ends when the body dies, he asserted that "whatever heaven mortal man may ever know is Here and Now, during the normal span of health." The 1948 typescript version of his autobiography reiterated that the soul, like the intelligence, was a "brain product" which terminated "when the vital chemism of the body's battery runs out." Far from being terrified by the prospect of annihilation, de Forest was comforted. The certainty of his total extinction, he said, freed him from fruitless speculation about the hereafter.[25]

De Forest was not always forthright in his disbelief. He spoke of God when writing to pious friends; he did not seek to disillusion people who obtained comfort from faith; and in 1953, when combatting godless communism, he even accepted the honorary presidency of the National Go-to-Church Campaign. But these were temporary expedients. In 1935 he looked forward to a time when "a genuine religion," stripped of superstition and dealing with man's relationship to man, not God, would dominate the human heart. While visiting Mexico in 1944, he observed that religion in that country was a major and profitable "industry." In time, he said, "science, of which I seem here to be *the* great exponent, will change all this." In 1957, four years after urging Americans to go to church, he described himself as an agnostic.[26]

In his later years de Forest curtailed his research, refraining from night work and allowing himself more recreation. He exercised strenuously: camping, hiking, and mountain climbing. In 1937 he made his first ascent of Mount Whitney, the highest peak in the forty-eight states; on 26 August 1943, his seventieth birthday, he scaled it for the fifth and final time. Age finally forced him from the mountaintops, but he remained vigorous. In his seventies he did not walk about the house but ran, and he jumped up stairs three at a time.[27]

Lee de Forest was nothing if not energetic. As a journalist described him: "Tall and thin, pinched cheeks stretched taut by high cheekbones, blue eyes burning in deep sockets, he seems all nervous energy, ever in danger of exploding or burning himself out." A friend of the inventor also resorted to electrical metaphor, calling him "a dynamo without much insulation." De Forest could not help operating at full force; restraint was not in his nature. When he watered the garden, he turned the hose on full-blast, much to the detriment of delicate plants. Lee de Forest could not let up.[28]

Not even on reading. In 1953 he read (or at least bought) books by Bunyan, Lamb, Macaulay, Anatole France, Henry Rider Haggard, and, most of all, Herbert Spencer. At about the same time, he asked a dealer to procure works by Plutarch, Shakespeare, Milton, Defoe, Cooper, Hawthorne, Prescott, Longfellow, Emerson, Poe, Tennyson, Kipling, and Renan. (Apparently the octogenarian had little interest in recent or contemporary literature.) He and Marie studied Spanish together. His grammar was good, she observed, but not his pronunciation. They also went to the movies. At comedies—de Forest especially liked Stan Laurel— the inventor would laugh so hard that he would distract the audience, making them laugh also. Sometimes Marie got so embarrassed that she would move several seats away.[29]

After three previous ordeals, de Forest's fourth marriage proved one long refreshment. Sharing her husband's fondness for nature and the arts, eager to please him, Marie filled all the requirements of the Golden Girl. She was beautiful, and she knew that her "latin heart" satisfied her "lusty" husband. For a time she worried that she could not provide all the "mental interest" that the inventor might desire—"St. Joseph and all the saints in Heaven help me," she implored—but soon it occurred to her that

she was proficient in foreign languages while he needed help.
Hence they took Spanish lessons—a chance for her to keep him
company of an intellectual sort.[30]

De Forest in turn adored her and tried to pamper her. When
first married, he hired servants to do the housework and wanted
his wife only to play the piano or write a book. Financial problems
soon restored cooking and cleaning to Marie's list of duties, but de
Forest continued to show consideration toward her. He took her
along on his travels, always sharing the limelight of his success,
and he spent on her whatever money he had. Once, when he
could not decide which of two fur coats to buy her, he took them
both. In 1958 he gave her a photograph of himself using a
compass to draw a circle. "A circle," he wrote on the picture, "has
no end, like my love for your own dear self." For all this Marie was
grateful. In the 1950s, when she worked on her autobiography, "I
Married a Genius" (never published), she declared herself lucky to
have such a husband.[31]

Seventy-seventh birthday. Lee and Marie at a surprise party in 1950, the year
he published his autobiography, *Father of Radio*. Photo courtesy of Perham
Foundation.

Marriage to a genius, however, had disadvantages. His scorn for conventions, for ordinary etiquette, caused his wife embarrassment, if nothing else. When tired of company, for instance, the inventor either retired suddenly to his study or simply told his guests to go home. Once, when addressing a club to which Marie belonged, de Forest bluntly told the group that he had been inveigled into coming and did not wish to come again. On another occasion he urged a woman to go on a diet, saying, "I was really amazed, yesterday, to see how much you had gained in weight since our last comparatively recent visit."[32]

An awesome tactlessness was not the only ill consequence of de Forest's egocentricity. Another was stubbornness. In 1952, when seventy-nine years old and partially deaf, he insisted on driving his own car. Even after having an accident, he angrily refused Marie's offer to act as his chauffeur. "That's right," he told her, "try and make an old man out of me . . . I'm not going to give up my independence just to coddle you." Marie responded by threatening to have his license revoked—and by admiring his pep.[33]

Some qualities, however, she could not admire. An unidentified typed page that appears to come from Marie's projected autobiography suggests several sources of intense strain on the marriage. During the Great Depression, the manuscript fragment reports,

> we were beseiged [sic] from every side for payments, pay on our car, silver, on which we had borrowed money—the counter-irritant[s] were the everpresent law suits, nerve wracking and wearing—our business threatened to be taken from us, our home—

Not all the troublesome lawsuits concerned patents: one of the nastiest involved Mrs. Henrietta Tilghman O'Kelly, de Forest's former mistress in New York. In 1931, after the inventor had gone west and married Marie Mosquini, O'Kelly sued him for breach of contract. She claimed that de Forest had guaranteed payment of the long-term lease on her apartment but had reneged. Then, allegedly in despair over de Forest's defaulting, she committed suicide. The following year her mother renewed the lawsuit. De Forest claimed he had paid O'Kelly thousands of dollars and owed her no more. The court apparently agreed, but not until after what Marie later reported as "day after day in court on the witness stand trying to clear him—of a penthouse lease where he lived with his mistress." That was no way to begin a marriage.[34]

After mentioning the O'Kelly lawsuit in her projected auto-biography, Marie de Forest had strong words about her husband:

> he has a trait—of when he needs one no more to ruthlessly cast them aside—he has become callous over the passing years till I verily believe a nail penetrating his heart could not be felt[35]

Marie never completed her memoirs. How could she publish such acidulous criticism in a book titled "I Married a Genius"?

But somehow she loved him. He called her "Mama"; she called him "Daddy." When he was featured on a television program in 1954, Marie beamed as she told the host that her twenty-four years of marriage had been "perfectly wonderful." She cared for the inventor during his final illness, and later she said that she knew what it meant to be willing to die for someone. In a sense, indeed, she *had* died for him, abandoning the limelight of Holly-wood and living in his reflected glory instead; finding in his life the meaning of her own. After the inventor died, his widow took it upon herself to sanctify his memory. Once, when a graduate student writing a dissertation about de Forest asked Marie "what the guy was like," she admonished him for disrespectfully refer-ring to Dr. de Forest as "the guy." By 1975 she had nothing ill to say about him and seemed entirely to have forgotten what she had written a quarter century before.[36]

In his autobiography de Forest reported that his marriage disappointed him in only one way: it was childless. Actually Marie had carried two children but had lost them both. After the death of one of them, a boy, she could hardly stand her husband's dismay. Lee de Forest would have no son to keep his name in remembrance.[37]

Over the years, de Forest maintained good relations with his three daughters, though not with his former wives. He wrote to his offspring and sent them money, receiving in return letters to "Dearest Dad" (from Harriet), "Precious Papa" (from Eleanor), and Dearest Daddy" (from Marilyn). When the girls had families of their own, he sent presents to his grandchildren.[38]

He did not correspond with Nora Barney, though they even-tually overcame the bitterness with which they parted. In the late 1950s their daughter Harriet brought the two together for a luncheon in Greenwich, Connecticut; and according to Nora's daughter Rhoda, Lee talked and laughed so much with Nora that his current wife, Marie, looked a bit left out. In 1958 the recon-ciliation was complete enough so that Lee said Nora could be counted on to cooperate with the possible production of a film about him.[39]

With Mary Mayo, in contrast, relations remained so hostile that he referred to her simply as "Mayo." His third wife had continued her alcoholic ways. In 1936, after throwing dishes at Marilyn during a drunken fit, she was persuaded by two policemen and a priest to send the eleven-year-old to a convent (Eleanor had already gone away to a Catholic school). Mary finished out her life in poverty and solitude. In 1951, when she was out of work and finding it difficult to live on the twelve hundred dollars a year she received from de Forest, her attorney wrote to him, asking for a voluntary increase in support. The former husband refused, suggesting that she seek aid from the state. Sometime thereafter Mary Mayo de Forest fell asleep while smoking in bed, set her mattress on fire, and died of asphyxiation.[40]

Meanwhile, de Forest's life assumed a tranquil regularity. Each morning he rose at seven—he was very punctual, his wife recalled—exercised, and ate a breakfast consisting of corn muffins, two poached eggs, and milk. Perhaps remembering certain pledges he had made when a boy, he forswore coffee and cigarettes. He did, however, have an extraordinary liking for peanut-butter-and-jelly sandwiches. After working at his lab, he would return each evening to the Hollywood home that he had named "Cielito Lindo," pretty little heaven.[41]

In the last decade of his life, de Forest seems to have thought often of his childhood motto, "to be a blessing." Although he could not perform philanthropy on the grand scale he had once planned, he depleted his modest earnings to benefit mankind. Yale University, flood victims in the Midwest, the Save the Children Foundation, the New York Metropolitan Opera, Mount Hermon School, a widow who could not meet a mortgage payment— to all these he made contributions. Marie de Forest believed that the primary motive behind all her husband's actions, including his inventions, was the desire to help others. When he saw a cripple hobbling down the street, for instance, he would try to think of something that science could do for the lame. When Marie's mother was dying in 1944, de Forest maintained a steady program of soothing music on the record player.[42]

While de Forest played benefactor to the world, the world rewarded him with distinctions. In 1930 he was elected president of the Institute of Radio Engineers. Eight years later the Federal Theater of the Air (the radio division of the Federal Theater Project) produced a play about him, one in a series on "Immortals

The father and his electronic "child," ca. 1950. The inventor examines an early Audion. Photo courtesy of Perham Foundation.

of Science." September 22, 1939, was Lee de Forest Day at the New York World's Fair. The American Institute of Electrical Engineers awarded him "my most cherished honor," the Edison Medal for 1946, for achievements in radio and for the invention of the Audion. In 1951 he was invited by Talladega College to deliver the commencement address. His accomplishments won recognition at two events in 1952: a testimonial dinner at the Waldorf-Astoria, with Herbert Hoover as the featured speaker, and the founding of the De Forest Pioneers (modeled after the Edison Pioneers), a group of veteran radio men who met yearly thereafter on de Forest's birthday to honor their former associate. In 1956, fifty years after de Forest invented the triode tube, a plaque was erected on the site of his New York laboratory. The following year he appeared on Ralph Edwards' TV program, "This Is Your Life." In 1958 the town of his birth, Council Bluffs, Iowa, dedicated Lee de Forest Elementary School.[43]

Too little, too late. Although the inventor took pleasure in the accolades, he did not find full satisfaction. The years of obscurity and loneliness, the frustration, the suffering, had engendered in him a bitterness that tainted each taste of glory. A few days before he received the Edison Medal, Marie asked him whether he was excited. No, he said: he felt resentment and anger at his fellow engineers' prejudice and jealousy which had deprived him for so long of the well-earned honor and had robbed him also of a Nobel Prize. Despite all the medals and banquets, de Forest never felt that he had received his fair share of recognition. Sometimes Marie would observe him sitting silently, staring at nothing, tense, angry, fuming over some past injustice. "He was like a piece of steel," she said, "they'd beaten him so much."[44]

As he moved through the eighth decade of his life, de Forest began to run down. He grew partially deaf and had a cataract in his left eye. In 1953 he showed evidence of heart strain, and his physician advised him not to climb hills or stairs. He was hospitalized with pneumonia in 1955, a syncope in 1957, and a bladder operation in 1958. After the second spell of heart trouble, he had an elevator installed at Cielito Lindo and went to bed earlier at night. On his eighty-fourth birthday he told the Associated Press that he hoped to live for ten years more.[45]

7

Father of Radio: 1950

"I have come to the conclusion," Lee de Forest told a prospective biographer in 1953, "that you have not done justice to the last ten years of my life." The biography emphasized "the bad luck which pursued me until recent years," paying little attention to later felicity. This was a mistake, because the reading public had a keener interest in success stories than in hard-luck stories. "I think, therefore," said the octogenarian, that more should be written about

> my later years, picturing the large handsome home in which I have lived, very happily married, since 1931—outlining among other things, the exceptional merits of my wife . . . I certainly did not want to be pitied by your readers—I should not be because my life on the whole has been full of grand triumphs and the last years have been notably comfortably tranquil—and your story should leave a happy impression with your readers.

In de Forest's own eyes, his life story had a happy ending.[1]

Certainly that was the way he himself described it. He had begun writing an autobiography in 1902, but it was not until the thirties that he worked on it in earnest. He produced lengthy manuscripts in 1933, 1939, and 1948, finally publishing *Father of Radio* in 1950. After thinking for nearly five decades about the meaning of his life, he succeeded at last in getting his thoughts into print. His self-portrait was not of a victim but of a conqueror.[2]

Not a haphazard collection of anecdotes, the book is the product of design. De Forest was proud of his writing; and in March 1949, as he revised the manuscript, he described his labors metaphorically. All he could do, he said, was to "re-dress and doll-up" his past. Like an architect conducting the public through a castle he had built long ago, he would show to his readers his life's achievements. But, aware of defects here and there, he would not allow the tourists to peer around a false panel or to take a step where a stone was missing. The autobiography had a clear purpose, and the author did not intend to cloud it with inconvenient facts.[3]

As the son of a preacher and teacher, and as a man intent on being a blessing to mankind, de Forest never scorned the didactic. In the preface to *Father of Radio,* he said that he wrote "in the hope that a frank revelation of my own struggles, disappointments, and successes may encourage others to embark on a similar career of discovery and invention." Lingering shade of Longfellow! By being a great man, Lee de Forest could inspire others to make their lives sublime. By frankly revealing his greatness, he would reform the world.[4]

Perhaps the most obvious theme of *Father of Radio* was the efficacy of Will. De Forest declared that his main purpose in writing the book had been to instill in American youth "courage, persistence, industry, and the ability to overcome all obstacles." To inspire young people to great achievement, he had recounted his own problems—technical, financial, and personal—showing how through sheer determination, he had surmounted them all. The last page of the book quotes Alexander Graham Bell's statement that "it is not you but circumstances that will determine your work," then goes on to refute it:

> In spite of circumstances, always most unfavorable, I hewed out the way I had mapped for myself—against poverty, despite adversity, cynical skepticism, and endless discouragement, and without adequate tools, financial or other. Looking back today the course I have followed, spite of fate and love and hate, seems incredible. But I had the vision, inner faith in myself, the inflexible resolve, the all-so-necessary courage.[5]

And he believed it. Ever since childhood, when he read the Biblical story of Joseph and deduced that "diligence is always rewarded," de Forest believed that unremitting effort would result inevitably in fame and fortune. His father reinforced his opinion. "By hard, persistent & steady work," he said, "you can accomplish wonders." The boy took these words of wisdom and pasted them in his journal. Many years later he said that "one thing only" was constant in his life: "battle, struggle, ambition, work." De Forest took pride in the will power that allowed him to labor so intently. In 1891 he said, "I stick to a thing like a seed tick." After finishing graduate school, he congratulated himself for fulfilling his resolution to work hard and steadily. Two decades later he read carefully a declaration by one Buxton (perhaps English social reformer Sir Thomas Buxton) that the difference between "great" men and "insignificant" ones was "energy—invincible determination, or a purpose once fixed and then victory or death." In the book that carried this quotation, de Forest underlined the words *energy, invincible,* and *purpose once fixed.*[6]

If invincible determination brought success, then fate did not exist. Bad luck, difficult circumstances, might retard one's progress temporarily; but if one only persisted, triumph was assured. In 1895 de Forest contracted typhoid; and while recuperating, he chanced upon a poem that he was not soon to forget. It was William E. Henley's "I. M. [In Memoriam] R. T. Hamilton Bruce":

> Out of the night that covers me,
>   Black as the Pit from pole to pole,
> I thank whatever gods may be
>   For my unconquerable soul.
>
> In the fell clutch of circumstance
>   I have not winced nor cried aloud.
> Under the bludgeonings of chance
>   My head is bloody but unbowed . . .
>
> It matters not how strait the gate,
>   How charged with punishments the scroll,
> I am the master of my fate:
>   I am the captain of my soul.

Years later de Forest would quote those last lines and scoff at weaklings who resigned themselves to fate or providence or chance. As an agnostic, he would not expect assistance from anything as uncertain as "whatever gods may be"; as the master of his fate, he would rely instead on his own "unconquerable soul." "We are," he would say in *Father of Radio,* "what we make ourselves."[7]

De Forest was self-consciously and proudly a self-made man. Self-made men were, he said, "the only real noble-men of the world; belonging to the only class whom I revere or respect." In 1905, when Abraham White suggested that wireless had "made" de Forest, the inventor retorted that it had not. Rather, he said, he had made wireless the vehicle on which he had risen. "When we speak of these matters Mr. White," he said, "we are getting pretty close to our inmost thoughts, and deepest principles . . . Unless you would wound me most deeply, do not intimate that wireless, or yourself, or any other lucky chance, or accident, 'made me.'" It was *he* that had made him, and not anyone else.[8]

If Will was one theme of the autobiography, Individualism was another. De Forest and the men he admired did not stubbornly defend old and popular ideas, but courageously promulgated new and unusual ones. In *Father of Radio* he portrayed early wireless men as pioneers spurred on by the challenge "of traversing new lands, of overcoming strange new obstacles, of doing what no one had done." The Daniel Boones of radio and talking pictures had ignored complacent doubters, had struggled against the immense inertia of the communications and movie industries, and finally had transformed the world. "Tradition, early teaching, the 'point of view,'" he said, "may all be wrong—were usually proven so to be." If progress were to continue, young Americans would have to leave the rutted highways and carve out paths of their own.[9]

Ever since childhood, when he revolted against parental discipline, de Forest had been something of an individualist. At Yale, however, as he read literature and philosophy, he reinforced his rebellious temperament with an antinomian ideology. On his desk calendar he scribbled such Emersonian slogans as "Insist on yourself—never imitate" and "Whoso would be a *man* must be a non-conformist." When he read Ibsen, "an enemy of all convention," he yearned "to throw off the lie and sham I am living." He wanted to be as great as Abraham Lincoln or Nikola Tesla, but rather than copy them, he wished "to bring out the truth that is *in me*."[10]

In 1911, de Forest wrote a poem that epitomized in a symbol the self-reliance he cherished. Entitled "The Lone Tree of Tamalpais," it described a huge old redwood which stood in solitude on the steep western slope of Mount Tamalpais in California. Far above its "clustered brethren," the Lone Tree stood as a monument to nonconformity and endurance:

> Through centuries of storm, through summers numberless
> Thy arrow shaft, thy vernal feathered blade
> Has shot aloft, nor dared the gale the less
> Because thy kinsmen in the valleys grouped their shade.

To de Forest, who usually hiked alone because no one could keep up with him, the tree imparted "a strength which shall not fail."[11]

As an individualist, de Forest hated to have bosses or even colleagues. In 1897, when a graduate student, he longed to be in "*agreeable* buisness, *my* buisness," where he would not have to worry about interference from others. As long as he could muster sufficient capital to support research, de Forest ran his own show. Rather than enlist in the ranks of AT&T or GE or RCA, he created De Forest Wireless and De Forest Phonofilm. Even in old age he managed to maintain a small laboratory in Hollywood financed by others but directed by himself. Only when there was no alternative, as in Chicago in 1899 or Palo Alto in 1911, would he serve as a hand in someone else's factory. Sure of his genius and intent on proving himself, de Forest disliked taking orders from superiors or sharing credit with peers.[12]

But if he was temperamentally suited to play the role of the lone wolf, he offered an intellectual justification as well. He acknowledged that huge industrial corporations, with armies of engineers and millions of dollars for research, seemed to provide great opportunity for invention; but their very size, he believed, ultimately retarded progress by stifling individual initiative. Few men in a big organization, he said in 1930, would call attention to themselves by doubting scientific orthodoxy, particularly if it meant disagreeing with their superiors in the company hierarchy. Thus, while the giant laboratories might contribute minor improvements to technology, the "epoch-making" inventions would continue to be made by the lone inventor. Ordinary minds should join the organization, he said, but the genius should work alone.[13]

Edison said the same thing. So did Reginald Fessenden, one of de Forest's radio rivals. But the future lay with the organization men, those like Michael Pupin—inventor, Columbia University professor of electrical engineering, and, coincidentally, teacher of both E. Howard Armstrong and Nora Blatch de Forest. "It is not so much the occasional inventor who nurses a great art like telephony and makes it grow beyond all our expectations," Pupin said in 1924, "as it is the intelligence of a well-equipped and liberally supported research laboratory." While an individualist like Fessenden opposed the creation of the National Research Council in 1916, saying that invention could not be planned and organized, the cooperation-minded Pupin believed that the council represented "the mobilized scientific intellect of the United States." While de Forest spoke of *making* epochs, Pupin (who called AT&T "the most perfect industrial organization in the world") talked of *nursing* arts.[14]

In the twentieth century the lone inventor, who could not possess thorough technical knowledge of every relevant aspect of a project, proved no match for the industrial corporation's team of experts. De Forest might invent the triode, but it took a team of AT&T engineers, some of whom were abreast of the latest discoveries in electronic theory, to make the thing work. According to Gerald Tyne:

> The manifold problems encountered were almost incapable of solution in any reasonable time by any one individual. It was only in the industrial laboratory where each problem could be attacked by a specialist that the desired result could be attained.

The versatile individual was supplanted by the group of specialists. This was evident in the radio industry, where, after the First World War, the lone wolf was nearly exterminated. According to Rupert Maclaurin, individual entrepreneur-inventors like de Forest, Marconi, and Fessenden guided the industry until the 1920s, but then were superseded by the large corporations.[15]

Nor was it just in the radio industry. Leonard Reich has shown that companies with well-funded industrial laboratories, like General Electric and Bell Telephone, had "significant advantages" over ones without them, thus making matters "exceedingly difficult for independent inventors." Likewise, Thomas Hughes has shown how the independents dominated invention between 1870 and World War I but thereafter were displaced by industrial scientists as the "principal locus" of research and development. The lone wolves continued to make more than their share of breakthrough inventions: e.g., air conditioning, the helicopter, the jet engine, the Polaroid Land camera, and Xerography. Nevertheless, Hughes observes, the independents never regained their old status as the main source of invention, nor did the public lionize them like Edison or the Wright brothers.[16]

Sometimes de Forest seemed to realize that the days of rugged individualism were over. In 1931, for instance, he said that with "gigantic industrial trusts" sponsoring thousands of researchers, the inventor would never again have Edison's chance to explore a field alone. In the galaxy of science, men like Faraday and Maxwell shone as bright as solitary stars; the anonymous multitude of the future were clusters of smaller suns; and "Lee de Forest was on the border space between!"[17]

Usually, however, de Forest denied that isolated luminaries were to be seen no more. In *Father of Radio,* he claimed that he himself had discovered a whole new "Invisible Empire of the Air" and that opportunities for invention were as great at mid-century as at the beginning. Betraying no suspicion that a swarm of scrub pines had supplanted the Lone Tree, he exhorted the youth of America to emulate his nonconformity.[18]

Father of Radio, then, was a hymn to Will and Individualism. De Forest strove consciously to inculcate these virtues in his readers. But he had yet another purpose in writing the book, a purpose of which he probably was not fully aware. If the autobiography was a paean to Will and Individualism, it was also a song of praise for the willful individualist Lee de Forest. From cover to cover it glorifies the pilgrim whose progress it so artfully delineates.

The eulogy begins on the dust jacket. The blurb on the back lists fourteen "Heroic Firsts in the life of Lee de Forest." Of these, some (such as "World's First three-electrode vacuum tube") are undoubtedly true and important. But most are either debatable ("World's First feedback, or oscillator, circuit") or trivial ("World's First broadcast of grand opera") or simply false ("World's First transmission of voices without wires"). Dust-jacket copy, of course, is not known for its veracity and restraint, and the publisher rather than the author may be responsible. But the text of the book itself is no less extravagant. De Forest fills one full page of the introduction with quotations praising himself, then goes on to relate his courageous struggle against stupendous obstacles and implacable foes. "I had discovered," he says, "an Invisible Empire of the Air, intangible, yet solid as granite, whose structure shall persist while man inhabits the planet . . . fading not as the years, the centuries fade away." Perceiving radio to be "solid as granite"—like a tombstone—he believed that it would last forever. And Lee de Forest was the Father of Radio.[19]

Or so he said. De Forest invented the triode and may be credited also with the feedback circuit, but this does not necessarily make him father of radio. To begin with, even his claim to have invented the vacuum tube is not beyond dispute. In England, Ambrose Fleming's homeland, it is the Fleming Valve, not the Audion, that is generally considered the ancestor of all the later electron-discharge tubes. Indeed, in England most of those tubes are *called* "valves," following Fleming's terminology. No one denies that de Forest took a big step in inserting a third electrode into the tube; but even that step was not the last, definitive one in the process of invention. Harold Arnold at Western Electric (and, at about the same time, Irving Langmuir at General Electric) recognized what de Forest did not: the need for a high vacuum in the tube. Only after the industrial laboratories of great corporations had modified the triode in important ways did it become the foundation of the electronics industry. Indeed, when the first high-vacuum triode amplifier went into commercial service in 1913, it was used in the telephone, not the radio. This shows how far the invention had gotten away from Lee de Forest. If the diode was invented by Edison but discovered by Fleming, the triode was invented by de Forest but discovered by Arnold and Langmuir. As Hugh Aitken says, the "hard" vacuum tube

> was significantly different from de Forest's audion. It had uses and functions that had been no part of de Forest's original objectives. And it operated according to scientific principles that he had great difficulty in accepting and that were certainly not the principles by which he thought the audion worked when he invented it. The invention changed drastically during the process of invention.

The invention of the vacuum tube was not a single act, occurring at a particular moment, but a process which extended over time and in which many inventors participated. "One ends up thinking of invention," says Aitken, "as, so to speak, plastic or malleable, and of the process by which the invention is made as essentially social or cooperative."[20]

If it is hard to assign an individual inventor credit for a single technical device like the vacuum tube, imagine the difficulty in ascribing paternity for an entire system like radio, which depends on *many* such inventions. De Forest's work on the vacuum tube was, no doubt, essential; but where would radio be without, say, Marconi's work on antennas and tuning devices? Unlike a human baby, an invention as big as radio has many "fathers."[21]

De Forest's failure to achieve the fame of an Edison or a Bell is due in part to his living at the beginning of an era in which even the greatest inventors produced only parts of a machine, not the complete and functioning thing. The public could light their houses with Edison's bulbs or talk over Bell's telephone, but what could they do with de Forest's Audion? An inventor does not become famous by producing something that people do not know they are using. Therefore, if he wishes to acquire renown, he does not call himself father of the three-electrode vacuum tube; he calls himself father of radio. Ironically, this emphasis on radio obscures his contribution to the vastly grander field of electronics.

De Forest's claim to the fatherhood of radio is no stronger from a commercial and organizational standpoint than from a technical one. Although his manufacture and sale of apparatus, his broadcasts, and his vigorous publicity campaigns no doubt stimulated the radio industry, he was far overshadowed in this regard first by Marconi, then by a more anonymous throng led by Owen D. Young and David Sarnoff of RCA. De Forest's radio companies never exerted the influence of the Marconi companies and RCA.[22]

But de Forest's claim to fatherhood is weakest where his work was weakest—at the level of theory. All the inventions of de Forest, Marconi, Fessenden, et al., would have been impossible without discoveries made by less practical men. Michael Faraday suggested that ether waves existed; James Clerk Maxwell formulated a theory of electromagnetism; Heinrich Hertz first produced and detected electromagnetic waves; J. J. Thomson discovered the electron. It is significant that Maclaurin, who calls the Audion "the most important single invention in the history of wireless," considers *Hertz* the father of radio—and Marconi the midwife. The first of Hugh Aitken's two volumes on the history of radio, the one dealing with "Origins," terminates at a time when the triode was still "over the horizon."[23]

Yet de Forest did not hesitate to claim the fatherhood of radio. It was a distinction which he felt he deserved and which he craved for decades. One day in 1920, as he listened to his radio receiver, he "realized suddenly & like a blow" how little credit he had received for being "*the* pioneer in the radiotelephone." Despite his "*big* & epoch-making invention" (the Audion), his name was not commonly associated with radio, not like Marconi's. Nor did he receive much in royalties. He admitted it largely was his own fault. He never should have sold his patents to AT&T but should have exploited them himself. "My conceit," he said, "was too small—I took too little pride in my achievement, was too willing to let it grow without my name." Ever after, he would regret doing what had seemed at the time to be a necessity, and he would seldom show a dearth of pride.[24]

Ever since youth, de Forest had longed for fame. In 1891 he recorded in his diary a resolution not to "live & die & world be as bad as it was & not know I ever lived—they shall know & be glad & sorry when I die—so help me God." What underlay such ambition, such a desperate hope for glory? One motive is suggested by a journal entry he wrote while in graduate school. He did little but "grind," he said, because he knew that he was preparing for "the near future of *supposed,* at least, appreciation." Ever since his father had chastised him, Talladega boys had bullied him, college classmates had shunned him, and professors had admonished him, Lee de Forest had been badly in need of a little "appreciation." To be a great inventor would provide him with precisely that. In 1906, at the tenth reunion of his college class, he was introduced amid yells from men who had heard of his work in wireless. "It was sweet," he said, "to feel the hearty hand-shakes, the frank words of appreciation & pride from classmates willing to honor me for what success I have achieved." But if recognition for a few wireless experiments was sweet, a general acknowledgment of his fatherhood of radio would be indescribably delicious. De Forest's quest for fame was an attempt to obliterate the bitter taste of hostility and indifference that he had endured through the years. Thus, invention was a kind of revenge.[25]

But there was more to it than that. If glory answered social needs, it fulfilled religious ones as well. As one disinclined to bend his knee in worship, de Forest could never rest assured that the true worth of each human being was as a creature and instrument of God. Dismissing Christianity as a collection of childish fables, he looked elsewhere for justification of man's existence—more particularly, of Lee de Forest's existence—for assurance that his life had meaning in a context larger than the present. He found that justification in greatness. If a man were not to be "insignificant" (to use Buxton's term), he would have to be "great." Longfellow's "great men," the sort who left "footprints on the sands of time," reminded de Forest that he too could make his life "sublime." In a post-Christian era, greatness brought immortality.

Theoretically, de Forest might have looked back on his career, noted the important inventions, felt confident that he had done great things, and contentedly ignored contrary opinion. A great man, certain of his work's lasting importance, need not worry whether his contemporaries appreciate it. De Forest, however, never had such confidence. All his life he hungered for prizes, honors, recognition of his greatness. Although an individualist, he needed reassurance from the crowd. *Father of Radio* was one more attempt to wring applause from a hitherto unappreciative audience. If the book brought him fame, he could feel more of the sweet assurance that his life had not been utter vanity. If he could convince the public, he could more easily convince himself.

Greatness was one path to immortality, but de Forest explored others as well. One which intrigued him especially was fatherhood. Ever since youth, when he kept a journal with the intention of reading it years later to his children, he dreamed of being a parent. On 6 May 1891, for instance—when he was seventeen—be began an entry with "Well Dear Children today I did as usual." In later years, when he actually produced progeny, he saw in them an immense significance. A devout materialist and a biological determinist, he believed that his offspring—drawn from his body, developing according to the immutable laws of genetics—perpetuated himself. When Harriot was an infant, he investigated her personality to discover characteristics inherited from himself (he found scientific curiosity, intelligence, imagination, and a sense of humor). While Eleanor was in Mary's womb, he wondered "whither and how will the stream of life carry our child?"

> A little, only little, can be altered after birth. *Now* thru the germ of my body, and the blood and soul of the mother, is the Future forming. Nine months and the years of *our* earlier lives have formed the mold of his destiny. His life is "his own," but we twain have formed it.[26]

Denying the existence of an afterlife, de Forest believed that a man lived on (in a quite literal sense) through his children. In 1911 he imagined a day when his daughter Harriot would have a baby and find herself "immortalized in my Grand Child." As he watched Eleanor sleep one night in 1923, he felt "the reality of hereditary life—the great solemn fact of fatherhood." To know that his daughter linked him to posterity made him feel intimate with "the great Immortality." Since he had created her out of himself, he lived as long as did she or her progeny. But de Forest was not just a materialist: he was also an evolutionist, and one with a millenialist bent. When his offspring inherited his qualities, it was no isolated and purposeless event, but part of some grand, portentous process. In the presence of his slumbering child, he could sense "the great, endless, vaguely dark future—indefinitely glorious." As he told his mother, he had a point of view somewhat different from her Christian one, but he shared her faith in "an Omnipotence infinitely above the mind of Man, and in the divinity of our evolution."[27]

Through his chromosomes, then, de Forest participated in the glorious future. Literal, biological fatherhood brought him a measure of immortality. But the notion of paternity was so appealing to him that he used it metaphorically also. During the first administration of Grover Cleveland, de Forest wrote a poem that was published in a church newsletter and preserved in his scrapbook. It was a survey of American presidents and began this way:

> First in the list is George Washington
> Father of his Country though he had no son.

De Forest repeatedly read his old diaries, so he may have remembered this couplet decades later when, with three daughters but no sons, he applied to himself the epithets "Father of Broadcasting" and "Father of Radio." Since, as he believed, radio was a great blessing to mankind and a contribution to progress, he would achieve through his electronic "child" the immortality of a Washington.[28]

Intent on greatness, desperate for fame, de Forest saw little but what lay between himself and his goals. A willful individualist, he fixed his attention on *his* purposes, *his* needs, *his* destiny. His way of operating an automobile might symbolize his general conduct. He drove the same way that he walked: at full speed, with eyes straight ahead, looking neither to left nor right, proving a menace to motorists or pedestrians who sought to cross his path.[29]

De Forest's self-centeredness made him place a high value on loyalty, not so much his loyalty to others as theirs to him. Unable to imagine that his associates had valid purposes that might contradict his, he judged them according to their conformity to his will. One electrician, for instance, followed de Forest's instructions to the letter, "and so we got along fine." With engineer Charles V. Logwood of Federal Telegraph, he had a little more trouble. Logwood at first seemed jealous and resentful of the newcomer to the company, but after acquiring "respect and admiration" for the inventor of the Audion, he became de Forest's "intimate" friend. As for early wireless operators, "their loyalty to wireless and to 'Doc' was at all times absolutely reliable, unswerving." These were the men who were "pioneers all."[30]

When de Forest read a magazine article entitled "Definitions of 'A Friend,'" he clipped it out and saved it. He put a check mark beside several of the definitions, including "A watch which beats true for all time and never 'runs down'" and "A bank of credit on which we can draw supplies of confidence, counsel, sympathy, help, and love." He did not put a mark beside "One who loves the truth and you, and will tell the truth in spite of you."[31]

De Forest's inclination to interpret all actions in terms of his own purposes resulted in the conviction that if his associates did anything harmful to him, they were guilty of treason. In 1906, for example, as his first marriage and his wireless telegraph company collapsed simultaneously, he wailed that most of his supposed friends were "broken reeds." "Every face is a mask," he said. "Deceit, artifice, untruth are the ingredients of human clay." Lucile Sheardown and Abraham White were not simply persons whose interests did not coincide with his, nor even fools, but "traitors, ingrates . . . deceivers beyond belief." The slings and arrows of outrageous fortune seemed to strike only from behind. Thus, when de Forest looked back on his career in 1950, he observed that the greatest threat to his success had not been the inherent difficulty of engineering problems, nor even the forthright opposition of commercial rivals, but rather the treachery of "sinister false friends boring from within."[32]

As this rhetoric suggests, the paranoid style that distinguished de Forest's politics extended also to his personal life. Everywhere he looked he found conspiracy and sedition. When newspapers questioned the soundness of Phonofilm stock, it was because they were instigated by the "devilish machinations" of William Fox or some other mysterious interest group "downtown." When the "Jewish judiciary" ruled against de Forest in a patent suit, it was because the judge had been bought. De Forest could imagine neither that his opponents were right nor that they were sincere in their error. Anyone who foiled him was a traitor or a crook.[33]

As he had intended, Lee de Forest left footprints on the sands of time. To his surprise, however, he found that people were not paying them much attention. In 1938, when Gleason Archer published his long–definitive *History of Radio,* de Forest's picture was opposite page 6, but Marconi's was on the frontispiece. In 1945, when Rupert Maclaurin asked for comments on a paper he had written about de Forest, the inventor found the historian's assessment "wrong," "wholly wrong," and *"Vicious."* In 1951, when *Newsweek Magazine* published an article on Yale University and the great men it had produced (for example, Noah Webster, John C. Calhoun, Samuel F. B. Morse), it neglected to mention de Forest, much to his amazement. As a stunt to generate publicity for de Forest's autobiography, his publisher addressed a letter to "the Father of Radio/Hollywood, California" in the hope that de Forest, upon receiving the letter, could tell the press how he had received a letter with so short but sufficient an address. The post office, however, failed the test. Unable to identify the Father of Radio, they returned the letter to its sender. Despite the inventor's achievements, fame never came his way. Not enough of it, anyway.[34]

In the final decade of his life, de Forest sought to rectify that injustice. His main weapon in this publicity blitz was his autobiography. De Forest had long been dissatisfied with what had been written about him, even by his admirers. In 1929 he tried to get a "well-known and capable writer" to produce "a real serious biography" of himself but was disappointed with the result.

Georgette Carneal's authorized biography of him, published in 1930, utterly failed, he said, "to grasp the real character, or scope, or the inherent *richness* of her subject." In 1945 two men were working on a biography (never published), but de Forest feared that it would be dryly factual "and lacking in the personality touch which would make it interesting to the greatest number of Americans." If he wanted the job done right, he would have to do it himself. So in 1950 he published *Father of Radio.*[35]

Publishing was not enough. It was necessary also to sell. Eager for wide distribution, de Forest personally took out ads in newspapers. He sent free copies to influential people and even to randomly selected members of the American Radio Relay League. He wrote to magazines, suggesting that they review the autobiography, and to bookstores, advising them to stock up. He asked a friend to suggest to *Readers Digest* that it reissue the book in condensed form, and he hired a press agent to prod the media. Despite all this, the book sold poorly. In 1952 more than half the five thousand copies printed remained on hand, a fact which de Forest attributed to the publisher's lack of enterprise in promoting the book.[36]

Although the book did not succeed, de Forest pressed the campaign on other fronts. He negotiated (unsuccessfully) for a movie depicting his life, and he instigated society-page editors to interview his wife. De Forest's press agent also kept busy. She wrote to a congressman, asking passage of a bill awarding de Forest the Medal of Merit, and to Hedda Hopper, suggesting that de Forest be a guest on her radio program.[37]

One of the main objectives in the war against obscurity was a Nobel Prize. Marconi had received one in 1909; why should the *true* father of radio be denied? The honor was overdue, to be sure, but better late than never. In 1952 de Forest asked a friend to try to get Irving Langmuir, winner of the 1932 Prize in Chemistry, to nominate de Forest for the physics prize. Nothing came of this, perhaps because Langmuir had sided with Howard Armstrong in the regeneration controversy and had doubted that de Forest fully understood how a vacuum tube worked. But in December 1954 Hugo Gernsback, publisher of *Radio-Electronics,* wrote to de Forest, saying he planned to print an editorial supporting him for a Prize. Finding this information "surprising, and extraordinarily gratifying," de Forest suggested campaign tactics. In March 1955 *Radio-Electronics* sounded the trumpet, and the war was on. Thomas J. Watson, chairman of the board of IBM, came out in de Forest's behalf. So did Charles Edison, former governor of New

Jersey and the son of Thomas Edison. When Gernsback wrote to Ernest O. Lawrence, the 1939 Nobel laureate in physics replied that he would be "more than glad" to support de Forest for having done work of "inestimable importance." Not everyone was so cooperative. Ernst F. W. Alexanderson and Alfred N. Goldsmith, two prominent engineers, refused to write the Nobel Prize committee.[38]

De Forest sought support in unlikely places. He asked a woman who had friends in Sweden to see what she could do; and when one of his advocates turned out to be a communist, de Forest decided that in this particular case, politics was not important. Gernsback asked that readers of *Radio-Electronics* send their letters of support to the magazine, but many readers wrote directly to the Swedish Academy instead, deluging that body with demands from the scientific proletariat. But the Academy was not impressed. The 1955 Nobel Prize in Physics went to Polykarp Kusch and Willis E. Lamb for their precise measurement of electromagnetic properties of the electron. The 1956 prize went to William Shockley, Walter Brattain, and John Bardeen for their development of the transistor—the device that supplanted de Forest's vacuum tube at the heart of electronics.[39]

One way for de Forest to brighten his own prestige was to dim that of his rivals. When Marconi died in 1937, de Forest wrote to the New York *Times,* praising Marconi as "father of the wireless telegraph" but denying him credit for the radio. In *Father of Radio* de Forest ridiculed Ambrose Fleming, his opponent in patent litigation, by pointing out sarcastically that despite adverse court rulings, the inventor of the Fleming Valve "never yielded in his firm conviction that he was radio's true inventor!" De Forest saved his most pointed jibes, however, for Howard Armstrong.[40]

De Forest had always hated the younger man: in 1920 de Forest called him "my *nemesis*—the 'poor boob' of Radio." In subsequent years the two men of science fought frequently and ferociously in courts of law, disputing title to the invention of the regenerative circuit. Armstrong lost the legal battle with de Forest, but that was only one in a long series of defeats, both professional and personal. Finally, on 31 January 1954, he opened a window in his Manhattan high-rise apartment and leaped out. When de Forest read the obituaries, he was shocked: they were much too complimentary. To correct the record, he wrote to *Scientific American,* saying that Armstrong had been self-centered, truculent, and resentful:

He seemed totally unreconciled to the fact that fate had denied him much that he had sought to achieve . . . As the years of his life extended and darkened, more and more gloomy appeared his outlook, until in bitterness he could endure no longer to face a warrior's future.

Replying to a writer who had called Armstrong a hero, de Forest said that he could not classify as a hero one who, rather than face "a turmoil, disaster, and frustration of his own making, chooses the easier escape of suicide."[41]

If de Forest described accurately Armstrong's despair, it was because he knew the feeling well. Despite all his optimistic talk, despite his genuine hopefulness, de Forest too had moments of terrible doubt. Ever since childhood he had found himself in the "dark place" of frustration and despair. Yet he always persevered: endured prolonged misfortune, stoked his hopes ever higher, refused to believe that fate could deny him his reward. The last word in his autobiography was *courage*. When Armstrong committed suicide, de Forest saw the fate that he had overcome.

Yet there was one destiny he could not avoid. By 1959, in the middle of his ninth decade of life, de Forest's heart ailments had become severe. Unable to sustain his usual vigorous activity, he lay in bed all day, cared for by his wife. He was nearly blind and, as a friend reported in 1960, "very weak, with everything out of control." In the early summer of 1961 he suffered a bladder infection. On 30 June he died. Up until the last week of his life, he thought he might pull through.[42]

Long before his death, de Forest planned the bequest of his collected writings. He offered his journals and sundry other manuscripts to Yale, but the university proved insufficiently enthusiastic. In 1955, therefore, he gave them to the Library of Congress. After de Forest's death, his wife donated his remaining papers and other artifacts to the Perham Foundation, which installed them in the Foothill Electronics Museum, on the campus of Foothill College, at Los Altos Hills, California. The museum, opened in 1973, featured a bust of the inventor, several of his early Audions, and an entire room devoted to the permanent display of his memorabilia. Thereafter thousands of schoolchildren and radio buffs filed through the museum to learn about the father of radio. In 1991, however, after a dispute between the Perham Foundation and Foothill College, the Electronics Museum

DeForest
Audions

U.S.
11c
AIRMAIL

Progress in Electronics

Stamp issued in 1973, the hundredth anniversary of de Forest's birth but twelve years too late to soothe his soul. He would have been pleased to be recognized as a contributor to "progress." Photo by Manuel Pereira.

was obliged to leave campus. Although a few of de Forest's memorabilia continue to circulate on temporary loan and display around the Bay Area, the bulk of the De Forest Memorial Archives reposes, little disturbed, in boxes in a vacant factory in Sunnyvale.[43]

De Forest left this world as penniless as he entered it. His prolonged illness had exhausted his savings, and in his last months he needed help. When he was no longer able to work, Bell Laboratories stopped sending his monthly retainer for consulting; but when informed that the inventor was in dire need, the company started sending the checks again. RCA and GE gave money for his care, and more came from his old associates in De Forest Pioneers. The man who had intended to become a millionaire and use his money "to be a blessing" to the less fortunate ended up on the receiving end. There was irony, too, in seeing the proud lone wolf of invention, the apostle of individualism, survive on donations from the great corporations against which he had so often railed. Lloyd Espenschied, noting the assistance to de Forest from big business, mused, "I wonder if 'Doc' will appreciate it; he was ever 'carniverous' " [sic]. One more time, the organization buried the man. When de Forest died, his entire estate consisted of a few last paychecks from Bell Labs.[44]

He had no funeral and was interred with simple rites performed by a Catholic priest. Thirty-five people attended the ceremony. All that was mortal of Lee de Forest lies buried in the cemetery of the San Fernando Mission in California.[45]

Source Abbreviations

DMA   De Forest Memorial Archives
LD   Lee de Forest
LDP   Lee de Forest Papers, Library of Congress, Washington, DC
MMD   Marie Mosquini de Forest

Notes

Introduction: Lives of Great Men: 1890

1. Aitken, *The Continuous Wave: Technology and American Radio, 1900–1932* (Princeton: Princeton University Press, 1985), 162–249; Tyne, *Saga of the Vacuum Tube* (Indianapolis: Howard W. Sams & Co., 1977).

2. Charles D. Cashdollar, *The Transformation of Theology, 1830–90: Positivism and Protestant Thought in Britain and America* (Princeton: Princeton University Press, 1989), 13, 18.

3. Robert V. Bruce, *Bell* (Boston: Little, Brown, 1973), 232–33; Matthew Josephson, *Edison* (New York: McGraw-Hill, 1959), 437–38; John J. O'Neill, *Prodigal Genius: The Life of Nikola Tesla* (New York: Ives Washburn, 1944), 9–10, 260–61, 263, 288; Tesla, *My Inventions: The Autobiography of Nikola Tesla*, ed. Ben Johnston (Williston, Vt: Hart Brothers, 1982), 29, 34, 36, 53–54, 105–7.

4. Oliver Lodge, *Past Years* (London: Hodder & Stoughton, 1931), 11, 14, 17; W. P. Jolly, *Sir Oliver Lodge* (Rutherford, NJ: Fairleigh Dickinson Press, 1974), 76; Michael Pupin, *From Immigrant to Inventor* (New York: Scribner's Sons, 1924), 105–7; W. P. Jolly, *Marconi* (New York: Stein & Day, 1972), 7, 151, 258, 263; Degna Marconi, *My Father, Marconi* (New York: McGraw-Hill, 1962), 277; Lawrence Lessing, *Man of High Fidelity: Edwin Howard Armstrong* (Philadelphia: J. B. Lippincott, 1956), 37; J. T. MacGregor-Morris, *The Inventor of the Valve: A Biography of Sir Ambrose Fleming* (London: Television Society, 1954), 106, 108.

5. Tesla, *My Inventions*, 27, 61; Josephson, *Edison*, 435; Marconi, *My Father*, 202, 204.

6. Bruce, *Bell*, 79, 256–57, 294, 354; MacGregor-Morris, *Inventor*, 106–7; Jolly, *Marconi*, 221, 236.

7. Bruce, *Bell*, 47, 189; O'Neill, *Prodigal Genius*, 243; Jolly, *Marconi*, 26; Marconi, *My Father*, 228–29; Lessing, *Man of High Fidelity*, 287–99; Thomas P. Hughes, *American Genesis: A Century of Invention and Technological Enthusiasm 1870–1970* (New York: Viking, 1989), 143, 149–50; Tom Lewis, *Empire of the Air: The Men Who Made Radio* (New York: HarperCollins, 1991), 327.

8. Orrin E. Dunlap Jr., *Marconi* (New York: Macmillan, 1937), 198; Bruce, *Bell*, 333–34; O'Neill, *Prodigal Genius*, 274; Inez Hunt and Wanetta W. Draper, *Lightning in His Hand: The Life Story of Nikola Tesla* (Hawthorne, CA: Omni Publications, 1964), 155.

9. Oliver Lodge was a rare historical phenomenon, an exception who proved the rule. Like most other inventors, Lodge lost the faith of his childhood; but unlike the others, he did not come to rely heavily on his inventions as vehicles to overcome death. Instead he became a convinced and proselytizing spiritualist, believing that the dead still lived and could even communicate with the living through mediums. Historian George Basalla has observed that although Lodge had the scientific and technical skill to create a commercially successful wireless system, he lacked the ambition to do so; and Lodge himself noted that he tended to wander off before finishing projects and that his life was marked more by drift

than ambition. He deplored arguments over priority and credit for inventions, and he concluded his autobiography by saying that although he had not reached his early goals, he was contented "to be used by Higher Powers to bear testimony to truth." Lodge had enough hunger for personal achievement to become an important inventor, but not enough to become one of the first rank, a Marconi. Cf. Basalla, *The Evolution of Technology* (Cambridge: Cambridge University Press, 1988), 99–100; Lodge, *Past Years*, 112–13, 338, 342, 352.

10. Lee de Forest (henceforth LD) to Henry S. De Forest, 4 October 1890, box 2, Lee de Forest Papers (henceforth LDP), Manuscript Division, Library of Congress, Washington, D.C.

11. The second quoted stanza should read: "Footsteps, that perhaps another, / Sailing o'er life's solemn main, / A forlorn and shipwrecked brother, / Seeing, shall take heart again." Longfellow, *Poetical Works*, 1 (Boston: Little, Brown, 1893), 20–22. For Longfellow's passion to go endlessly onward (and upward— "Excelsior"), see William E. Bridges, "Warm Hearth, Cold World: Social Perspectives on the Household Poets," *American Quarterly* 21, no. 4 (Winter 1969): 774–75. For the poet's repeated spells of "darkness" and his resort to "a life of action and reality," see Newton Arvin, *Longfellow* (Boston: Little, Brown, 1963), 49–50, 117–18, 306.

12. De Forest was not unique among men of his time. At the funeral of Alexander Graham Bell in 1922, a Presbyterian minister recited "A Psalm of Life." Cf. Bruce, *Bell*, 493.

Chapter 1: An Enduring Record for Fame: 1893

1. Henry always spelled the family name with a capital D, but sometime between 1884 and 1889 Lee switched to the lower case. Cf. correspondence in box 1, LDP.

2. Undated obituary of Anna De Forest from *The American Missionary*, 744, box 2, LDP; *National Cyclopaedia of American Biography* 35 (New York: James T. White & Co., 1949), 337; LD, *Father of Radio: The Autobiography of Lee de Forest* (Chicago: Wilcox & Follett, 1950), 11–12; Addie L. J. Butler, *The Distinctive Black College: Talladega, Tuskegee and Morehouse* (Metuchen, NJ: Scarecrow Press, 1977), 18.

3. LD, *Father*, 400; ca. 19 March 1907, Journal 18, pp. 60–61; 26 December 1926, and 26 January 1927, both Journal 23; Lewis, *Empire of the Air*, 205. LD's twenty-three journals are in the LDP.

4. Maxine D. Jones and Joe M. Richardson, *Talladega College: The First Century* (Tuscaloosa: University of Alabama Press, 1990), 42, 43, 65.

5. LD, *Father*, 13; clipping from letter from Henry to Lee, pasted at back of Journal 3.

6. Henry De Forest to Theodore Dwight Woolsey, 4 April 1865, Woolsey Family Papers, Yale University Manuscript Collections; unidentified obituary in box 1800, De Forest Memorial Archives (henceforth DMA), Electronics Museum of the Perham Foundation; *The Talladegan* 35, no. 2 (January 1918): 6, in scrapbook, DMA. When the author examined the DMA in 1975, they were at Foothill College, Los Altos Hills, Calif. As of November 1991, however, they were in a vacant factory in Sunnyvale, Calif. The vicissitudes of time and motion have probably affected the precise location of documents within the collection; so

when the author in his footnotes cites specific folders and boxes in the DMA, he does so with more optimism than confidence.

7. Jones and Richardson, *Talladega*, 13–16, 63–64; Henry De Forest to William L. Kingsley, 2 August 1890, Kingsley Memorial Collection, Manuscripts and Archives Division, Yale University, New Haven, Conn.

8. Rev. A. F. Beard and Treasurer E. C. Silsby, in *The Students' Idea* 5, no. 5 (April 1904): 2, 5–6, in box 2, LDP; Jones and Richardson, *Talladega College*, 56–62.

9. LD, *Father*, 29, 41.

10. "The Diaries of Doctor De Forest," TMs dated 1939, p. 35, De Forest Family Papers, Yale University, New Haven, Conn.

11. *Statistics of the Population of the United States at the Tenth Census*, vol. I (Washington: Government Printing Office, 1883), 98; 7 January, 28 March and 2 April 1891, Journal 1; LD to "Grandma," 12 January 1884, box 1, LDP; LD to Anna De Forest, 5 July 1887, in scrapbook, DMA.

12. LD, *Father*, 5, 23–27; Georgette Carneal, *A Conqueror of Space: An Authorized Biography of the Life and Work of Lee De Forest* (New York: Horace Liveright, 1930), 14–18; LD, "A Fragmentary Study in Autobiography Written in 1902–1903," 5–9, TMs in box 1900 (1), DMA.

13. Carneal, *Conqueror*, 35–36; LD, *Father*, 36. It was not only American schoolboys who were trying to build perpetual motion machines at this time. Between 1855 and 1903, England issued more than 500 patents for such devices, and in 1911 the exasperated and exhausted U.S. Patent Office ordered that henceforth all applications for patents on perpetual motion machines must be accompanied by working models. Cf. Basalla, *Evolution of Technology*, 74.

14. Robert G. Sherer, *Subordination or Liberation? The Development and Conflicting Theories of Black Education in Nineteenth Century Alabama* (University, AL: University of Alabama Press, 1977), vii, 137–46; Joe M. Richardson, *Christian Reconstruction: The American Missionary Association and Southern Blacks, 1861–1890* (Athens: University of Georgia Press, 1986), 129–31; clipping from *Talladega College Record*, sometime in 1890s, in scrapbook; James D. Anderson, *The Education of Blacks in the South, 1860–1895* (Chapel Hill: University of North Carolina Press, 1988), 66–69, 243.

15. LD, *Father*, 45–46; Journal 1, n.p. Although named Talladega College in its charter of 1869, the school spent its first quarter century concentrating on primary and secondary education, preparing its charges for college-level work. It was not until late in Henry De Forest's presidency that Talladega introduced a full college course (1891) and produced its first college graduates (1895). Cf. Jones and Richardson, *Talladega College*, 43, 49.

16. 1 January and 3 June 1891, Journal 1; LD, *Father*, 53–54; MSS. in scrapbook and in box 2, LDP.

17. LD, "Fragmentary Study," 3; *Father*, 22, 27–28; 28 March and 17 April 1891, Journal 1.

18. Note by Anna De Forest, dated 26 August 1925, in scrapbook; Samuel Lubell, "Magnificent Failure" (a three-part series in the *Saturday Evening Post*, 17, 24, and 31 January 1942), 24 January: 75; 22 May 1891, Journal 1.

19. LD, *Father*, 29; 10 March and 30 April 1891, Journal 1.

20. Ibid., 6, 28–29.

21. Ibid., 28–29; Lubell, "Magnificent Failure," 17 January: 76; LD, "Fragmentary Study," 3–4.

22. 22 June 1906, Journal 17; 12 December 1916, Journal 19; 15 April 1921, Journal 21.

23. Clippings from letters from Henry to Lee, at the back of Journal 3; LD, "Father of Radio," TMs dated 1948 and much different from the *Father of Radio* published two years later, p. 142, De Forest Family Papers; LD, *Father,* 38, 40.

24. LD to Anna De Forest, 2 August and 14 September 1889, box 1, LDP; LD to same, 13 August 1889, in scrapbook.

25. LD to same, 13 August 1889, in scrapbook.

26. LD to —, ca. 14 September 1889, box 1, LDP; LD to Anna De Forest, 1 September 1889, in scrapbook.

27. LD to Anna De Forest, 1 September 1889, and *Talladega College Record* 4, no. 4 (February 1896), both in scrapbook; LD, *Father,* 31.

28. Henry to Cynthia De Forest, 26 August 1873, in scrapbook; "Diaries," 43–44.

29. 11 February 1891, Journal 1; Lubell, "Magnificent Failure," 17 January: 76.

30. "Diaries," 43–44.

31. 17 January 1891, Journal 1.

32. 7, 12, and 16 July 1891, Journal 1; LD, *Father,* 55–56; 3–28 August, Journal 2.

33. 1–3 September 1891, Journal 2; Lubell, "Magnificent Failure," 17 January: 78.

34. LD, *Father,* 56; 7 October 1891, Journal 2; 18 April 1892, Journal 3; 4 and 29 March 1893, Journal 4; 16 April 1893, Journal 5.

35. Journals 3–5, passim; 23 April 1893, Journal 5.

36. 24 October 1892, Journal 4; 29 May and 12–14 June 1893, Journal 5.

37. Report cards in box 2, LDP, and in scrapbook; 18 December 1891, Journal 2; 21 March 1892, Journal 3; 4 February and 4 March 1893, Journal 4; Charles E. Dickerson to LD, 26 July 1929, box 1, LDP; LD to Mrs. Charles Dickerson, 9 February 1939, box 1930 (2), DMA. One of the poems he wrote during these years was "The Land of the Cosine," a mathematical fantasy (MS in box 2, LDP).

38. 19 November 1892, and 4 February 1893, Journal 4.

39. Journal 1, passim; LD to Henry and Anna De Forest, 31 July 1892, box 1, LDP; LD to Anna De Forest, 21 August 1892, in scrapbook; LD, *Father,* 59, 62.

40. LD to Anna De Forest, 5 August 1891, in scrapbook; "Diaries," 76, 81; 25 June and 1 July 1892; 15 January, 3, 9, and 10 February 1893, all in Journal 4.

41. 24 March, 26 April, and 10 May 1891, Journal 1; 27 July 1892, Journal 4.

42. LD to Henry De Forest, March [n.d.] 1893, box 1800, DMA.

43. LD, *Father,* 48; LD to Henry De Forest, March 1893, box 1800, DMA. *Esse Benedictus* would be translated more accurately as "to be blessed" than as "to be a blessing." LD may have confused the two.

44. Undated clipping in scrapbook; 11 April 1892, Journal 3; LD, *Father,* 58–59.

45. Clippings dated 29 October 1892, and 29 May 1893, in scrapbook; 17 October 1892, Journal 4; 29 April 1893, Journal 5.

46. 16 April and 6 July 1893, Journal 5.

Chapter 2: I Wish to Excell: 1895

1. Lubell, "Magnificent Failure," 17 January: 78; 10 September 1894, Journal 7; 25 March 1895, Journal 8; 22 June 1896, Journal 10.

2. Note by Anna De Forest, 26 August 1925, in scrapbook; Lubell, "Magnificent Failure," 17 January: 78.

3. Lubell, "Magnificent Failure," 17 January: 78; 24 October 1896, Journal 11; 30 June 1897, Journal 12.

4. 20 November 1895, Journal 9; 5 June 1897, Journal 12.

5. 28 September 1895, Journal 9; 20 September 1896, Journal 10; 10 May 1897, Journal 12; 5 March 1898, Journal 13.

6. "Statistical Questions, Yale 96S" (a questionnaire distributed to seniors), box 2, LDP; undated newspaper clipping (probably ca. June 1895), in scrapbook; Lubell, "Magnificent Failure," 17 January: 78; Lloyd W. Smith to LD, 18 April 1895, box 1, LDP.

7. 8 April 1894, Journal 7; Palo Alto *Times,* 18 January 1951: 17; Carneal, *Conqueror,* 74; "The Progress in Aerial Navigation," *Yale Scientific Monthly* 2, no. 2 (November 1895): 55–57, 67; *Times* quoted in John Jewkes, David Sawers, and Richard Stillerman, *The Sources of Invention,* 2nd ed. (New York: Norton, 1969), 174.

8. 25 March 1895, Journal 8.

9. 28 December 1896, Journal 11; Aitken, *Continuous Wave,* 162.

10. 10 December 1893, Journal 6; 29 April 1894, Journal 7; 21 February 1897, Journal 11; 11 September 1897, Journal 12; 21 November 1898, Journal 13.

11. MS of Scientific Oration in box 2, LDP; 12 August 1894, Journal 7.

12. 26 and 27 August 1894, Journal 7.

13. Poe, *Memorial Edition of the Complete Works,* 5 (Boston: Desmond, 1902), 245–46; 9 November 1896, Journal 11. Later LD became disenchanted with Poe's philosophizing. Reading *Eureka,* LD found the mathematics and physics erroneous and lamented that Poe had lived too early to make use of the theory of evolution. Cf. 29 August 1897, Journal 12.

14. 26 August 1894, Journal 7; 22 September 1895, Journal 9.

15. MS in box 2, LDP; 20 May 1894, Journal 7; 14 March 1897, Journal 11; 2 September 1897, Journal 12.

16. 28 March 1891, Journal 1; 24 May and 13 June 1893, Journal 5.

17. 26 January–23 February 1896, Journal 9.

18. 25 November 1895, Journal 9; 4 July 1896, Journal 10; 20 August 1897, Journal 12; "Statistical Questions."

19. 3 April 1897, Journal 11; 20 August 1897, Journal 12.

20. "Father of Radio" (TMs), 105; 28 December 1896, Journal 11; 24 January 1925, Journal 22; LD to Anna De Forest, November [n.d.] 1924, box 1, LDP. By conflating the spiritual and the material, LD showed he had much in common with spiritualists. Cf. R. Laurence Moore, *In Search of White Crows: Spiritualism, Parapsychology, and American Culture* (New York: Oxford University Press, 1977), 22–26.

21. *The Talladegan* 68, no. 7 (June 1951): n.p., in box 2, LDP; 31 July 1891, Journal 2; 20 July 1892, Journal 4; 16 April 1893, Journal 5; 22 September, 2 October and 2 December 1893, Journal 6.

22. 25 December 1893, Journal 6; 9 April and 13 October 1894, Journal 7; 6 October 1895, Journal 9; 23 April and 15 June 1896, Journal 10; 15 February 1897, Journal 11; "Statistical Questions."

23. 30 June 1893, Journal 5; 2 March 1894, Journal 7.

24. 30 December 1895, Journal 9; 25 May 1896, Journal 10.

25. 15 May 1894, Journal 7; November–December 1894, Journal 8.

26. 4 February 1895, Journal 8.

27. 22 October 1893, and 11 February 1894, Journal 6; ca. August 1895, Journal

9; 25 May and 2 September 1897, Journal 12.

28. 23 December 1894, Journal 8; 4 July 1896, Journal 10.

29. 15 May 1896, Journal 10.

30. 21 February 1897, Journal 11; 29 August 1897, Journal 12.

31. 23 December 1894, Journal 8; 3 April 1897, Journal 11; LD to Harriot Stanton Blatch, 4 November 1936, box 1, LDP.

32. 9 July 1894, Journal 7; 28 September 1895, Journal 9; 5 October 1896, Journal 10; 3 November 1896, Journal 11.

33. Journal 1, n.p.; 16 August–14 September 1893, Journals 5 and 6; LD, *Father,* 62–63; Carneal, *Conqueror,* 54–56.

34. Rough draft of LD to Bryan, n.d., in scrapbook; Lawrence W. Levine, *Defender of the Faith: William Jennings Bryan* (New York: Oxford University Press, 1965), esp. 260–66.

35. 20 March 1899, Journal 13.

36. 3 June 1895, Journal 8.

37. Ibid.; 24 October 1897, Journal 12.

38. Cf. Richard Hofstadter, *Social Darwinism in American Thought* (Philadelphia: University of Pennsylvania Press, 1944); 24 October 1897, Journal 12; LD to Anna De Forest, 6 October 1912, box 1, LDP. For LD's reverence of TR, see scrapbook, in which he pasted letters to and from TR, plus newspaper clippings about him.

39. 22 July 1894, Journal 7; 3 June 1895, Journal 8.

40. For LD's later political activities and ideas, see chapters 4 and 5 of this book.

41. Howard Segal, *Technological Utopianism in American Culture* (Chicago: University of Chicago, 1985), 1; 20 January 1901, Journal 15.

42. 19 August 1894, Journal 7; 28 January 1895, Journal 8; 3 November 1895, Journal 9; ca. 4 August 1897, Journal 12; 26 February 1899, Journal 13; postcard in box 1, LDP.

43. 5–26 March, 26 and 28 April 1894, Journal 7; 31 January 1897, Journal 11; 22 March, 25 and 26 June, 6 July, and 19 August 1897, Journal 12; 25 January 1898, and 12 February 1899, Journal 13; newspaper clippings in scrapbook.

44. Ca. February 1896, Journal 9; 25 May, 3 and 6 July, 2 and 18 October 1897, Journal 12. The breakup, however, was not permanent. A year after it, LD reported that Lillian was "a dear good friend." Cf. 18 October 1898, Journal 13.

45. 20 November, 18 and 24 December 1893, Journal 6; 3 November 1895, Journal 9; Lubell, "Magnificent Failure," 17 January: 78; LD to G. I. Black, 23 March 1898, box 1800, DMA.

46. 10 May 1897, Journal 12; ca. September 1898, 1 and 20 November 1898, Journal 13.

47. Ca. 5 August 1895, Journal 9; Ca. 31 January and 22 February 1897, Journal 11; 13 May 1897, Journal 12.

48. 31 December 1896, and 15 February 1897, Journal 11; 3 October 1897, Journal 12; LD, *Father,* 400.

49. 4 and 5 January 1896, Journal 9; 11–19 January 1897, Journal 11.

50. 19 January–2 March 1897, Journal 11; 7 March 1898, Journal 13.

51. March 25 and June 3, 1895, Journal 8.

52. 11 February 1895, Journal 8; 25 February 1896, Journal 9.

53. 3 June 1895, Journal 8; 25 February 1896, Journal 9.

54. Calendar in box 2, LDP; 25 March 1895, Journal 8; 23 February 1896, Journal 9; 14 March 1897, Journal 11.

55. 3 November 1893, Journal 6; 18 April 1898, Journal 13.
56. 25 April 1898, Journal 13.
57. 2 May–15 September 1898, Journal 13.
58. 14 February 1898, Journal 13.
59. Ibid.; LD, *Father,* 72, 77.
60. 22 March 1891, Journal 1; sketch in DMA; 7 March 1898, Journal 13.

Chapter 3: The Driven Ones: 1904

1. 12 August, ca. late September and 26 November 1899, Journal 14; LD, *Father,* 101–06.
2. LD to Marconi, 22 September 1899, photostatic copy in DMA; Hunt and Draper, *Lightning in His Hand,* 129; 8 April 1900, Journal 14.
3. LD, *Father,* 108–12; Carneal, *Conqueror,* 96–105; 3 September 1900, Journal 14.
4. LD, *Father,* 113–115; 28 October 1900, Journal 14; 23 December 1900, and 10 February 1901, Journal 15.
5. LD, *Father,* 115–17; "Diaries," 192.
6. LD, *Father,* 120–22.
7. 23 December 1900, and 1 September 1901, Journal 15.
8. 1 September 1901, Journal 15.
9. Susan J. Douglas, *Inventing American Broadcasting 1899–1922* (Baltimore: Johns Hopkins University Press, 1987), 19–21, 56.
10. LD, *Father,* 123–26; 10 November 1901, Journal 15; Robert A. Chipman, "De Forest and the Triode Detector," *Scientific American* 212 (March 1965): 95; *Electrical World and Engineer* 38 no. 15 (12 October 1901): 596–97.
11. 22 December 1901, and 17 May 1902, Journal 15.
12. 15 December 1901, Journal 15.
13. 23 March 1901, Journal 15. Smythe seems eventually to have accepted his displacement, because by 1925 he was writing to LD in a friendly, nostalgic tone. Cf. Smythe to LD, 2 January 1925, in De Forest Radio Co. Correspondence, box 41, George Clark Collection, Archives Center, National Museum of American History, Smithsonian Institution, Washington, D.C.
14. Lubell, "Magnificent Failure," 24 January: 21; Carneal, *Conqueror,* 144.
15. Susan Douglas, "Exploring Pathways in the Ether" (Ph.D. diss., Brown University, 1980), 112–119.
16. 20 July 1902, Journal 15; 13 November 1903, and 5 July 1904, Journal 16. De Forest himself was known to pull a fast one on occasion. Once in about 1907 he and assistant Frank Butler were arranging a demonstration of wireless when Butler accidentally broke the transmitter. Faced with a humiliating public failure, Butler suggested stringing a concealed wire between the transmitter and the receiver and sending signals that way. "My God, Butler," exclaimed De Forest, "we could never do that. It would be against the law and we'd get prison if they caught us." Upon further reflection, however, de Forest conceded that "it's the only thing we can do. Go ahead!" The subsequent demonstration of "wireless" sold "quite a little stock," Butler later reported, and eventually helped de Forest sell sets to the Navy. Cf. Butler, dictating to G. H. Clark, "The Acquisition of the Wireless Telephone by the U.S. Navy," 10 December 1946, box 405, Clark Collection.
17. LD, *Father,* 140–42, 152–58. In his autobiography published after World War II, LD recollected that in 1904 it was the Japanese who silenced Lionel

James's transmitter. However, L. S. Howeth says that the Japanese permitted the broadcasts but the Russians, who were losing the war, protested to the British and American governments. Cf. Howeth, *History of Communications-Electronics in the United States Navy* (Washington: Government Printing Office, 1963), 74.

18. LD, *Father*, 165–81; 5 July and 18 September 1904, Journal 16.

19. 5 April 1903, Journal 15.

20. 14 July–12 August 1899, Journal 13; 11 September 1899 and 28 January 1900, Journal 14; Helen Brown to Hope Scrogin, 11 September 1970, box 11, De Forest Family Papers; LD, *Father*, 99–100; LD to Jessica Wallace, 9 August 1902, box 1900 (1), DMA.

21. 5 April 1903, Journal 15. Jessica survived and became a frequent correspondent of LD in the 1950s.

22. 27 May 1903, Journal 15; 20 August 1903, and 2 April 1905, Journal 16; "To Kathleen of the Bar," ca. 1902, in scrapbook; Nellie de Forest Gaskill to "Marie and Lee" [n.y. but probably 1904], in scrapbook.

23. 27 March 1904, Journal 16; 23 December 1905, Journal 17. Apparently he was not too familiar with the senator's daughter, for he spelled her name *McHenry*.

24. New York *Times,* 17 February 1906: 9; 18 February: 20; 5 October: 3 (the *Times* variously reports the bride's name as Lucille Sherdown, Lucile Sheardown, and Lucille Sheardon); Journal 17, p. 28; 11 March 1906, Journal 17.

25. 11 March and 22 June 1906, Journal 17.

26. 11 March, 19 July, and 10 August 1906, Journal 17; Journal 17, p. 15; New York *Times,* 5 October 1906: 3. Lucile disputed the charges, attributing the breakup of the marriage to Lee's "cruel treatment" of her, which as early as the honeymoon had become "well-nigh unbearable." Cf. New York *World,* 5 October 1906.

27. 11 March, April–June, and 19 July 1906, Journal 17; 13 February 1908, Journal 18.

28. White to LD, 26 August 1905, and LD to White, 28 August, in scrapbook; LD, *Father*, 184–85.

29. LD, "Diaries," 243; Gleason L. Archer, *History of Radio to 1926* (New York: American Historical Society, 1938), 81; LD, *Father*, 217; Douglas, "Exploring Pathways," 103, 260.

30. Reminiscences of Lloyd Espenschied, 1963, p. 3, Oral History Collection of Columbia University, New York; LD, *Father*, 217–20; 30 September 1906, Journal 17; LD to Mr. H—, 29 November 1906, Journal 18.

31. Inscribed at bottom of copy of letter to company directors, 28 November 1906, and quoted in Carneal, *Conqueror,* 166–67.

32. LD, *Father*, 113, 128; 31 December 1899, Journal 14; IOUs of 15 June 1899, and 24 February 1901, in scrapbook; LD to —, 2 March 1901, Journal 15; 30 September 1906, Journal 17.

33. LD, *Father*, 50–51, 128; LD to Jessica, 9 August 1902, box 1900 (1), DMA; LD, "Fragmentary Study in Autobiography."

34. Newton quotation in Journal 1, n.p.; Scientific Oration; LD, *Father*, 86; 2 September 1897, Journal 12.

35. James Turner, *Without God, Without Creed: The Origins of Unbelief in America* (Baltimore: Johns Hopkins University Press, 1985), 238–39.

36. 8 February 1898, Journal 13; 20 January 1901, Journal 15; "The Driven Ones," dated March 1904, MS in box ND (1), DMA.

37. Anna De Forest to LD, 26 August 1902, in scrapbook; LD to Jessica Wallace, n.d. but on stationery printed for 1902, box 1900 (1), DMA.

Chapter 4: *At Last, at Last:* 1907

1. Journal 1, n.p.; *The Poetic and Dramatic Works of Alfred Lord Tennyson* (Boston: Houghton Mifflin, 1898), 170, 175; 8 April 1900, Journal 14; 25 June 1907, Journal 18; LD (prob. to Dawson's Book Shop), 7 December 1953, correspondence file 1955–56 [sic], DMA. In his response to "Statistical Questions" in 1896, de Forest said that his favorite poet was Tennyson and that his favorite poem was "Idyls of a King" [sic].

2. LD, *Father*, 229–30.

3. 28 February and 5 March 1907, Journal 18. LD may have picked up the word from Nora Stanton Blatch, whom he had met just before he used it in his journal. Blatch and other suffragists applied the word *broadcasts* to the leaflets they distributed on streetcorners, and de Forest may have applied the term to the information he dispensed over the radio. In 1940 G. H. Clark asserted that as of 1907, U.S. Navy wireless telegraph operators commonly used the term *broadcasting* to mean "sending a message to several receiving stations without requiring any of them to acknowledge receipt"—messages such as time signals and weather reports. However, Clark's memory may have failed him. The present author examined the boxes in the Clark Collection dealing with Navy radio (series 100) but could find no document older than de Forest's 1907 journal which used the term. Moreover, Clark himself notes that during the Navy's round-the-world cruise of 1907–09 the operator who played phonograph records over the wireless reported in his log that he "gave out music," not that he "broadcast" it. A recent etymological dictionary says that the first use of *broadcast* as a noun and verb relating to radio was recorded in 1921. However, de Forest's use of the word as an adjective predates this by fourteen years. Cf. Ellen DuBois, "Spanning Two Centuries: The Autobiography of Nora Stanton Barney," *History Workshop Journal*, no. 22 (Fall 1986): 149; Clark, "The Development of Radio in the U.S. Navy," TMs, 1940, pp. 63–64, box 400, Clark Collection; Robert K. Barnhart, ed., *The Barnhart Dictionary of Etymology* (n.p.: H. W. Wilson, 1988), 119.

4. LD, *Father*, 248–49, 267–71.

5. Ibid., 232–35, 247–48; LD, "Progress of Radio-Telephony," *Electrical World* 53, no. 1 (2 January 1909): 13; Howeth, *History of Communications-Electronics*, 169–72; G. H. Clark, "De Forest and 'Navy Wireless,'" TMs., n.d., p. 1, box 404, series 100, Clark Collection.

6. Maclaurin, *Invention and Innovation in the Radio Industry* (New York: Macmillan, 1949), 58; Aitken, *Continuous Wave*, 217. Also see Archer, *History of Radio*, 93; LD, *Father*, 210–5l; and Herbert T. Wade, "Wireless Telegraphy by the De Forest System," *Review of Reviews* 35 (June 1907): 681–85.

7. Tyne, *Saga of the Vacuum Tube*, 30–34; Aitken, *Continuous Wave*, 205–7. My account of de Forest's part in the history of the vacuum tube depends heavily on the analyses by Tyne and Aitken, particularly the latter.

8. Tyne, *Saga of the Vacuum Tube*, 33–35; Aitken, *Continuous Wave*, 209–10.

9. Tyne, *Saga of the Vacuum Tube*, 40–42; Aitken, *Continuous Wave*, 211–12.

10. Tyne, *Saga of the Vacuum Tube*, 42–43.

11. Aitken, *Continuous Wave*, 214–15.

12. Tyne, *Saga of the Vacuum Tube*, 53–59; Aitken, *Continuous Wave*, 195–204.

13. Aitken, *Continuous Wave*, 204–5; Tyne, *Saga of the Vacuum Tube*, 53–55.

14. Aitken, *Continuous Wave*, 205, 213–14; Tyne, *Saga of the Vacuum Tube*, 61, 64.

15. Lewis, *Empire of the Air*, 53; Tyne, *Saga of the Vacuum Tube*, 61–62; Aitken, *Continuous Wave*, 216–19.

16. Aitken, *Continuous Wave*, 219–22, 547; Carneal, *Conqueror*, 191. The "audible ions" definition appears in De Forest Radio Co. advertising copy for a "Book of New Jersey," dated 28 August 1928, in De Forest Radio Co. Correspondence, box 41, Clark Collection.

17. LD, *Father*, 245.

18. 1 January, 26 February, and 17 March 1907, Journal 18; LD, *Father*, 222–25, and "Diaries," 342; DuBois, "Spanning Two Centuries": 149. In Poe's tale "Eleonora", the narrator and the story's namesake live in a valley through which flows the River of Silence. In 1910, after his breakup with Nora, LD wrote "Lost River: An Allegory," in which two streams, one from a Western land and one from England, flow side by side in a valley and are called "Leeonora" [sic]; merge briefly into a single River of Loving Lives; but then die out in a desert. Obviously LD remembered Poe's tale, and apparently its name charmed him because it combined Lee with Nora. By calling Nora "Leonora" he was naming her after himself, annexing her; but eventually she proved herself just plain Nora. Nevertheless, LD named his next child (by his next wife) Eleanor, showing his persistent attachment to the name. Poe's tale may have appealed to LD partly because of its sanctioning of abandonment. In the story the narrator loves Eleonora. As she is dying, he promises never to marry another and invokes a horrible curse upon himself should he ever break that promise. After she dies, however, he loves and marries "the ethereal Ermengarde." One night the spirit of Eleonora speaks to him and, much to his relief and surprise, tells him to sleep in peace, for "thou art absolved, for reasons which shall be made known unto thee in Heaven, of thy vows to Eleonora." In LD's own life he broke any number of commitments—to Jesus, teetotalism, his mother, the poor, various women—and probably felt relieved by the assurance that such "progress" might be forgiven, even blessed. LD's sense of guilt over his own betrayals may help account for his frequent accusations that other people—spouses, business partners, or communists—were turncoats. The noisiest patriot often has treason in his heart. Cf. "Lost River," box 2, LDP; "Eleonora," *The Complete Works of Edgar Allan Poe*, ed. James A. Harrison, vol. 4 (New York: AMS Press, 1965), 236–44.

19. 10 November 1900, Journal 14; 27 May 1904, Journal 18.

20. 1 January and ca. 10 September 1907, Journal 18.

21. Ca. 10 September 1907, Journal 18; New York *Times*, 20 January 1971: 38. The most thorough published biography of LD's second wife is Terry Kay Rockefeller, "BARNEY, Nora Stanton Blatch," in Barbara Sicherman and Carol Hurd Green et al., eds., *Notable American Women: The Modern Period*, vol. 1 (Cambridge: Harvard University Press, 1980), 53–55.

22. DuBois, "Spanning Two Centuries": 134, 149; LD to Nora, 18 and 31 January 1907, Journal 18.

23. 15 April 1907–ca. late February 1908, Journal 18; Lubell, "Magnificent Failure," 24 January: 38; New York *Times*, 26 February 1908: 7.

24. LD, *Father*, 237–40; "Diaries," 365.

25. Journal 1, n.d., n.p.; 24 October 1897, Journal 12; 11 April 1898, Journal 13.

26. 22 July 1894, Journal 7; "Statistical Questions"; 11 September 1897, Journal 12.

27. "Statistical Questions"; LD to Nellie de Forest Gaskill, ca. 10 September 1907, Journal 18; Rhoda Barney Jenkins, interview with the author, Greenwich, Conn., 23 February 1991. Mrs. Jenkins tells a story that illustrates the fixed

determination of her mother and, for that matter, of her father, Morgan Barney. When Nora gave birth to a son, Nora wanted to name him John, but Morgan preferred Peter. Neither parent would give in, so the baby's birth certificate bore no first name. All through his childhood his mother called him John, his father called him Peter, and his sister diplomatically avoided calling him anything at all. When the young man joined the merchant marine during World War II, the government required him to have a legal first name; so he chose John. This was prudent, for by this time his father had died but his mother remained very much alive. Nora and Morgan Barney had separated not long after the birth of the baby with no name.

28. LD, *Father*, 241, 243; "Diaries," 365.

29. LD, "Diaries," 370, and *Father*, 245–46, 251; LD to Nora, 11 August 1908, Journal 18.

30. LD, *Father*, 260. Although originally named Harriot after her maternal grandmother, LD's daughter had changed the spelling to Harriet by the time of her marriage. Wedding invitation in box 1930 (1), DMA.

31. 13 March–25 April 1911, from a group of entries titled "Leaves from the Diary of a Baby," TMs in box 1900 (2), DMA.

32. 24 April–8 May 1911, "Leaves from Diary"; undated pages clipped from a Rockefeller Foundation report, box ND (2), DMA.

33. LD to Anna De Forest, 5 June 1911, box 1900 (2), DMA.

34. LD to Nora, 18 March [prob. 1912], box 1900 (2), DMA; 18 June 1911, "Leaves from Diary"; New York *World*, 20 July 1911.

35. Nora went on to a career as an engineer, architect, and developer. In 1919 she married Morgan Barney, a naval architect, by whom she later had two children. She became a leader of the woman suffrage and peace movements, and in 1950 she was investigated by the House Committee on Un-American Activities. In 1957 she attempted to write her autobiography but carried it forward only until the time she met de Forest; the unhappiness of her marriage seems to have been too large and wild to reduce to words. Nora Stanton Barney died in 1971. Cf. DuBois, "Spanning Two Centuries": 132, 135; Rockefeller, "BARNEY": 54–55.

36. LD, *Father*, 253, 263–65, 272–76.

37. "Leaves from Diary," n.p.

38. LD, *Father*, 276–77, 289; 5 June 1910, Journal 19; LD to Anna De Forest, 15 October 1911, box 1900 (2), DMA.

39. New York *Times*, 28 March 1912: 1, LD, *Father*, 283.

40. LD to —, 29 March 1912, Journal 19; LD, *Father*, 311, 321. LD promptly and fully paid back contributors to his Defense Fund.

41. LD, *Father*, 311–14; New York *Times*, 1 January 1914: 1; 20 January 1914, Journal 19.

42. LD, *Father*, 300–1; *National Cyclopaedia of American Biography*, A (New York: James T. White, 1930), 19; 22 January 1913, Journal 19.

43. LD, *Father*, 277–78, 292–95; Carneal, *Conqueror*, 243–44; *National Cyclopaedia*, A, 19.

44. Maclaurin, *Invention and Innovation*, 78–79; Lessing, *Man of High Fidelity*, 67–73; Michael Pupin to Editor, New York *Times*, 10 June 1934: sec. 4, p. 5; Archer, *History of Radio*, 114. The de Forest-Armstrong controversy is explored thoroughly and convincingly in Lewis, *Empire of the Air*, 189–219. The quotations are from pp. 193–94.

45. Maclaurin, *Invention and Innovation*, 78; *RCA, AT&T, & De Forest v. Radio Engineering Laboratories*, 293 U.S. 1; *Father*, 375–82. After the 1934 decision, LD's

attorney expressed delight over "what a good patent judge Cardozo turned out to be on his first attempt. The fact that he wrote the opinion was a source of great amazement to me because all during the argument he gave me the impression of enjoying, and when I say enjoying, I mean enjoying, a sound sleep." Cf. Ed Darby to LD, 23 May 1934, box labeled "decide later," DMA.

46. Maclaurin, *Invention and Innovation*, 78–79n.; Lessing, *Man of High Fidelity*, 189–90, 285.

47. Stone to Samuel Lubell, 11 June 1941, box 313, Clark Collection; Aitken, *Continuous Wave*, 237–38.

48. Aitken, *Continuous Wave*, 243–45; Tyne, *Saga of the Vacuum Tube*, 86–87.

49. Aitken, *Continuous Wave*, 246; Lubell, "Magnificent Failure," 24 January: 43; Archer, *History of Radio*, 107.

50. LD, *Father*, 304–7.

51. Stone to Lubell, 11 June 1941, box 313, Clark Collection; LD, *Father*, 307–10; Lubell, "Magnificent Failure," 24 January: 43. Casting further doubt on the report of subterfuge by Sidney Meyers is the fact that de Forest repeatedly told how AT&T had underpaid him but without alleging any false representation by Meyers. Cf. LD to Philip F. Nowlan, 8 July 1927, LDP; and LD to C. K. Fankhauser, 3 December 1954, and 1 June 1956, in Theodore W. Case Archives, Cayuga Museum, Auburn, N.Y.

52. LD, *Father*, 310, 315.

53. Ibid., 316–44; memo by John J. Carty, 8 April 1909, quoted in N. R. Danielian, *A.T.&T.: The Story of Industrial Conquest* (New York: Vanguard, 1939), 104; Maclaurin, *Invention and Innovation*, 129; Leonard S. Reich, "Research, Patents, and the Struggle to Control Radio," *Business History Review* 51, no. 2 (Summer 1977): 212–13.

54. LD, *Father*, 337–39; 6 December 1916, Journal 19.

55. LD, *Father*, 341, 349–52.

56. Archer, *History of Radio*, 82, 92, 97, 115; Josephson, *Edison*, 281; Maclaurin, *Invention and Innovation*, 85. Fleming and LD argued their cases in the pages of the London *Electrician*, 30 November and 28 December 1906, 4 January 1907, 11 September, and 9 October 1908.

57. Maclaurin, *Invention and Innovation*, 85–87, 129–130; LD, *Father*, 322–26, 404–5; Reich, "Research, Patents, and the Struggle to Control Radio": 217–18.

58. LD, *Father*, 329–30, 342; copies of pamphlets in box 1900 (2), DMA; 8 April 1917, Journal 19; undated clipping from New York *Sun*, in scrapbook.

59. New York *Times*, 21 January 1916: 4; TMs of speech, LD to Editor of New York *Sun* (undated clipping), and Roosevelt to LD, 24 May 1916, all in scrapbook.

60. 10 September and 6 December 1916, Journal 19; LD to Anna De Forest, 10 November [1918], box 1900 (2), DMA.

61. Boston *Globe*, 21 March 1917: 6; LD to Anna De Forest, 19 May 1918, Journal 19; Liberty Bond receipt and undated clipping from *Musical Advance* in scrapbook.

62. Mary to LD, ca. November 1918, telegram in scrapbook; LD to Anna De Forest, 15 December 1918, box 1900 (2), DMA; 12 December 1916, and 24 January 1917, Journal 19.

63. LD to Samuel E. Darby Jr., 11 November 1932, box 1930 (1), DMA. See also Darby to LD, 15 November 1932, box 1930 (1), and Darby to LD, 29 May 1945, box 1940 (2).

64. LD to Mary, 27 November [1918], box 1800 [sic]; LD to Darby, 11 November 1932, box 1930 (1); MS of poem, box 1900 (2), all in DMA.

65. LD to Mary, 15 October and 8 December 1918, box 1900 (2), DMA; LD to

Mary, 20 October 1918, box 1, LDP; LD to Mary, 27 November [1918], box 1800 [sic], DMA; March–April 1919, Journal 19; 13 May, 24 August–3 September 1920, Journal 20; 24 April 1921, Journal 21.

66. 1 October 1919, Journal 19.

67. Ibid.; LD to Anna De Forest, 2 October 1919, box 1900 (2), DMA.

Chapter 5: I Can Steel My Heart: 1926

1. LD, *Father*, 358–59; LD, "The Phonofilm," *Transactions of the Society of Motion Picture Engineers*, no. 16 (May 1923): 62.

2. 2 February 1919, Journal 19.

3. Edward W. Kellogg, "History of Sound Motion Pictures," in *A Technological History of Motion Pictures and Television*, ed. Raymond Fielding (Berkeley: University of California, 1967): 175; LD, "Recent Developments in 'The Phonofilm,'" *Transactions of the Society of Motion Picture Engineers*, no. 27 (October 1926): 69; Kenneth Macgowan, *Behind the Screen: The History and Techniques of the Motion Picture* (New York: Delacorte, 1965), 280–81.

4. 2 September 1919, Journal 19; 3 January, 8 September, and 6 October 1920, Journal 20.

5. The case of LD does not support Andre Bazin's contention that the goal of "total cinema"—complete representation of reality, both auditory and visual— preceded the technological developments that made it possible. LD started using light to record sound even *before* he saw the technique's applicability to the movies. He sought high-fidelity music, not total cinema. Cf. Bazin, "The Myth of Total Cinema," in *What Is Cinema?,* tran. Hugh Gray (Berkeley: University of California, 1967), 17–22.

6. 15 September 1896, Journal 10; LD to "Mother and Sisters Mary," 6 October 1912, ct. 1, LDP; LD, *Father*, 306; 10 November 1920, Journal 20. For a technical description of LD's phonofilm system, see Kellogg, "History of Sound Motion Pictures": 177; LD, "The Phonofilm": 63–69; and LD, "Recent Developments": 65–68.

7. 9 July 1921, Journal 21; Miles Kreuger, "The Birth of the American Film Musical," *High Fidelity* (July 1972): 43; LD, *Father*, 369; LD to T. W. Case, 13 August 1920; 10 November 1920; and 22 September 1922, all in Case Archives; New York *Times*, 16 April 1923: 20. Peter Jones, director of the Cayuga Museum in Auburn, N.Y., is doing very promising research on Case, an important, interesting, and strangely neglected inventor.

8. 28 June 1920, Journal 20; 1 July 1923, Journal 21; LD, *Father*, 362, 372– 73; New York *Times*, 6 April 1923: 19; 22 May: 5; and 25 August: 13. The company went bankrupt in 1926, was reorganized, went bankrupt again in 1933, and had its assets bought by RCA (Maclaurin, *Invention and Innovation*, 86, 130; LD, *Father*, 404–7).

9. LD, *Father*, 370, 388, 391, 399; Macgowan, *Behind the Screen*, 281–82; New York *Times*, 13 March 1923: 12, and 5 April: 12; 13 January 1924, Journal 22. Many of de Forest's completed Phonofilms, tests, and out-takes are in the Maurice Zouary Collection at the Motion Picture, Broadcasting and Recorded Sound Division, Library of Congress, Washington, D.C. Historians will enjoy Al Smith singing about the Bowery and De Wolf Hopper reciting "Casey at the Bat."

10. 15 and 31 August 1924, Journal 22; Lee Nixon to LD, 26 August 1951, and LD to Nixon, 24 September 1951, in personal correspondence, DMA. In later years LD remembered these events very differently, recollecting Coolidge

as a sagacious statesman and Davis as a dishonest bungler ("Father of Radio," TMs, 965–66).

11. LD, *Father,* 387; New York *Times,* 19 September 1924: 3.

12. New York *Times,* 21 March 1924: 23; LD, "The Phonofilm": 75.

13. 10 February 1924, Journal 22; LD, "The Phonofilm": 67; Lubell, "Magnificent Failure," 31 January: 46; LD to Walter K. Long, 13 March 1958, Case Archives; Macgowan, *Behind the Screen,* 281.

14. Kreuger, "Birth of American Film Musical": 43.

15. LD, *Father,* 389, 396; Macgowan, *Behind the Screen,* 282–83; ca. July 1924, Journal 22.

16. LD, "Phonofilm Progress," *Transactions of the Society of Motion Picture Engineers,* no. 20 (September–October 1924): 17–19.

17. Ca. July 1924, Journal 22; LD, *Father,* 392–93; New York *Times,* 7 May 1925: 2.

18. New York *Times,* 9 May 1925: 19; 17 May 1925, Journal 22.

19. Kreuger, "Birth of American Film Musical": 43; Case to LD, 16 September 1924; LD to Case, 21 November and 5 December 1925, all in Case Archives; 19 December 1925, Journal 22.

20. 28 March 1926, Journal 23.

21. 15 August and 22 November 1920, Journal 20; Journal 21, passim; 13 January 1924, Journal 22; LD, *Father,* 362–66.

22. 20 January, 9 October and 7 November 1920, Journal 20; 5 June 1921, Journal 21; LD, *Father,* 371–72, photos opposite p. 391; LD to Anna De Forest, 16 September 1923, ct. 1, LDP.

23. March–April 1919, Journal 19; 28 November 1920, Journal 20; 2 June 1923, Journal 21; Journals 20–22 passim; LD, *Father,* 360.

24. 15 October, 1 and 7 December 1924, Journal 22.

25. Anna De Forest to LD, 22 August 1905; 31 March 1917; and 5 August 1922; note by Anna De Forest, dated 26 August 1925, all in scrapbook; 26 December 1926, Journal 23; LD, *Father,* 290–91, 305, 462.

26. *National Cyclopaedia of American Biography* 37, 190; clipping from *The World Magazine,* 6 July 1919, in scrapbook.

27. 4 April 1926, Journal 23; LD to Charles, 1 June 1931, ct. 1, LDP; Charles to LD, July [n.d.] 1932, box 1930(1), DMA; William H. Pouch to LD, 20 February 1951, box 1950 (1), DMA; LD, *Father,* 463.

28. New York *Times,* 21 March 1924: 23; quoted in Carneal, *Conqueror,* 210. While a desire to clean up the airwaves was de Forest's principal reason for speaking out, it was not his only one. In a letter to the publicity director of De Forest Radio in 1930, the inventor noted the public's favorable response to his crusade and urged the company to "take full advantage of this situation for helpful publicity." Two days later he added that the project "could be of direct value for building up the good name of De Forest" and be made "a very powerful factor for publicity of a most helpful nature, beneficial at once to the general cause of radio and also to the cause in which we are more directly interested." Cf. LD to Paul Staacke, 14 and 16 January 1930, in De Forest Radio Co. Correspondence, box 41, Clark Collection.

29. 13 January and ca. April 1924, Journal 22; LD, "Recent Developments," 74; "The Phonofilm," 73–75.

30. 25 July 1926, Journal 23; Kellogg, "History of Sound Motion Pictures," 180.

31. 25 July and 7 October 1926, Journal 23.

32. Macgowan, *Behind the Screen*, 283–84; Kellogg, "History of Sound Motion Pictures," 178–79; Lubell, "Magnificent Failure," 31 January: 46; Kreuger, "Birth of the American Film Musical," 43–44.

33. 26 December 1926, Journal 23; LD, *Father*, 396–97, 401–4; New York *Times*, 3 October 1928: 40.

34. 2 June 1923, Journal 21; 30 March 1924, Journal 22.

35. 1 November 1925, Journal 22; 15 April 1926, Journal 23; LD, *Father*, 394–95.

36. 29 November 1925, Journal 22; 4, 15, and 25 April, 2 and 9 May 1926, Journal 23.

37. 9 and 16 May 1926, Journal 23; LD, *Father*, 394.

38. Maclaurin, *Invention and Innovation*, 130; 11 June and 27 August 1927; 28 April 1929, and 30 August 1931, all in Journal 23; New York *Mirror*, 26 January 1931 (clipping provided by Tom Lewis); Miriam [no last name] to "Lee, mon bien aimé," 24 July 1930. See also Miriam to LD, 29 July, 5 and 22 August 1930, all in DMA, box 1930 (1).

Chapter 6: At Last, at Last: 1931

1. Marie Mosquini de Forest (henceforth MMD), interview with author, 21 January 1975, Hemet, CA; LD, *Father*, 408; New York *Times*, 10 October 1930: 18; New York *Herald-Tribune*, 11 October 1930 (clipping obtained by Tom Lewis). There is some question as to Marie's age. The *Times* and *Herald-Tribune* articles announcing the marriage both say she was forty-one. However, in numerous photos she looks much more than sixteen years younger than de Forest; and when this author interviewed her in 1975, she seemed much younger than eighty-six. Based on dates in her movie career, Tom Lewis guesses that she was about twenty-four in 1930. Pat Eickman's 1972 newspaper story based on an interview, "Love just like in the movies," says Marie was only seventeen when she married de Forest; but that figure is surely too low. On the other hand, a photograph published in April 1931 shows Marie de Forest as an amply mature woman who may indeed have been forty-one the previous year. So perhaps the newspapers were right after all.

2. Lubell, "Magnificent Failure," January 31: 48; Eickman, "Love just like in the movies"; Los Angeles *Times*, 3 June 1951: pt. 3, p. 8; LD, *Father*, 408–9; MMD interview. Mosquini was christened Maria but was renamed Marie by promoters.

3. Eickman, "Love just like in the movies"; LD to Charles de Forest, 1 June 1931, ct. 1, LDP.

4. New York *Times*, 19 July 1930: 1, and 27 July 1930: sec. 9, p. 11.

5. Joseph H. Udelson, *The Great Television Race* (University, Ala: University of Alabama Press, 1982), ix, 2, 51, 54, 55. By this time LD was only a consultant for De Forest Radio, with no direct role in its management.

6. LD, *Father*, 418–21, 435–38; New York *Times*, 5 January 1936: sec. 9, p. 15; Udelson, *Great Television Race*, x; Omaha *World Herald Magazine*, 2 April 1950: 5C–6C; Maclaurin, *Invention and Innovation*, 191–215.

7. LD, *Television: Today and Tomorrow* (New York: Dial Press, 1942), 35–41, 330–54. This book contains what may be another of LD's neologisms: "the broadcast, or telecast, as it shall be called to distinguish it from radio" (p. 186).

8. LD, *Father*, 423–32; LD to Dr. C. D. Ingham, ca. summer 1953, personal correspondence, DMA; Palo Alto *Times*, 18 January 1951: 17; *Dictionary of*

Scientific Biography 4, 7; Maclaurin, *Invention and Innovation,* 87.

9. Lewis, *Empire of the Air,* 291–295.

10. New York *Times,* 4 December 1936: 28; Palo Alto *Times,* 18 January 1951: 17; LD to Dr. A. J. Schramm, 23 April and 22 May 1951, and H. T. Swartz to LD, 4 May 1954, Foundation correspondence, DMA; LD to Harry Becker, 29 April 1958, personal correspondence, DMA; unidentified obituary in box 11, De Forest Family Papers.

11. George E. Brown to LD, 22 July 1944, box 1940 (2); LD to Social Security Administration, 16 February 1956, personal correspondence; LD to Gordon B. Greb, 14 February 1959, box 1950 (3), all in DMA; LD to Jessica Wallace Millar, 26 May 1952, box 11, De Forest Family Papers.

12. Chicago *Tribune,* 28 October 1946, quoted in LD, *Father,* 443–44; *Father,* 447–48; "The Cerfboard," *This Week Magazine,* 16 January 1955. The pun, drawing on the first line of Longfellow's "Evangeline," was originated by LD's friend George Clark. Cf. "Father of Radio," MS, 1126.

13. LD to Mary Ralph, Charles de Forest et al., 24 April [n.y.], box ND (1), DMA; LD to Harriot Stanton Blatch, 4 November 1936, ct. 1, LDP; LD to George Killenger, 18 November 1952; LD to Richard Nixon, 5 November 1952; LD to Joseph McCarthy, 7 December 1953; LD to the *Nation,* 31 December 1953, all in personal correspondence, DMA; *Yale Scientific Magazine,* October 1954: 7.

14. New York *Times,* 9 January 1930, 22; LD to West Virginia Society of the Sons of the Revolution, 30 June 1931, box 1930 (1), DMA.

15. LD to Charles de Forest, 12 March 1933, ct. 1, LDP (letter erroneously dated 1932 and filed accordingly, though internal evidence makes clear that it was written the following year); LD to Mary and Philip Ralph, May [n.d.] 1946, box 1940 (2), DMA; LD to Sen. William F. Knowland (with copies sent to all congressmen), 12 April 1949, box 1940 (3), DMA; LD to Editor of Los Angeles *Examiner,* 15 November 1951; LD to Douglas MacArthur, 21 November 1951; LD to Pat McCarran, 12 March 1953, all in personal correspondence, DMA; LD to Jessica Wallace Millar, 30 January 1953, box 11, De Forest Family Papers; Free Enterprise Foundation membership certificate in box 1950 (3), DMA.

16. Personal correspondence, 1950–1954 passim; LD to William E. Elliott, 23 November 1953, personal correspondence; LD to Marshall Neilan, 29 June and 31 August 1953, autobiography correspondence; LD to Hope, 15 and 23 June 1953, and Hope to LD, 20 June 1953, personal correspondence, all in DMA.

17. LD to George Vaughan, 2 August 1935, and LD to "sister and brother," 31 July 1932, both in ct. 1, LDP; "How New Years Came to Hollywood," MS in box 1930 (1), DMA. Americans won more than half the gold medals in the 1932 Olympics.

18. LD to Vaughan, 2 August 1935, ct. 1, LDP.

19. "Progress in Aerial Navigation": 67; "Progress in Aerial Navigation— 1934," *Yale Scientific Magazine* 9, no. 1 (Fall 1934): 21–22.

20. Michael S. Sherry, *The Rise of American Air Power* (New Haven: Yale University Press, 1987), 5, 23–24; Hughes, *American Genesis,* 101, 127.

21. Sherry, *Rise of American Air Power,* 6.

22. Summary of interview for *Colliers Magazine,* ca. January 1955, MS in box 1950 (2), DMA; LD, *Father,* 449; LD to Radio Free Europe, 5 September 1956, box 1950 (3), DMA. See also New York *Times,* 9 January 1930: 22 for an earlier statement of the same views.

23. LD, *Father,* 448; New York *Times,* 27 July 1930: sec. 9, p. 11; New York *Times,* 20 May 1923: sec. 8, p. 3; LD to American inventors at International Patent Exhibition, 8 September 1931, box 1930 (1), DMA.

24. New York *Telegram,* 27 January 1930: sec. 2, p. 1.

25. Los Angeles *Times Sunday Magazine,* 9 October 1932: 12–14; "Father of Radio," 1169–70.

26. LD to Jessica Wallace Millar, 22 February 1953, box 11, De Forest Family Papers; LD to Selby L. Collinson, 4 June 1957, personal correspondence; LD to Raymond Stewart, 27 August 1953, Go-to-Church correspondence; LD to "Folks," 17 June 1944, box 1940 (2), all in DMA; LD to George Vaughan, 2 August 1935, ct. 1, LDP.

27. LD, *Father,* 412–15; MMD interview.

28. Lubell, "Magnificent Failure," January 17: 10; MMD interview.

29. Dawson's Book Shop to LD, 7 December 1953, and LD to —, n.d., personal correspondence; undated note by MMD in box labeled "decide later," both in DMA; MMD interview.

30. Undated note by MMD, box labeled "decide later," DMA.

31. MMD interview; Pat Eickman, "Love just like in the movies," Riverside, CA, *Press,* 19 October 1972: C-1; TMs by MMD, 1952, box "decide later," DMA. In 1975 the inscribed photo was in MMD's possession.

32. Lubell, "Magnificent Failure," January 31: 48; LD to Mrs. Vera Hestmark, 30 September 1953, personal correspondence, DMA.

33. Ts fragment by MMD, dated 28 August 1952, box labeled "decide later," DMA.

34. New York *Mirror,* 26 January 1931 (clipping obtained by Tom Lewis); Lewis, *Empire of the Air,* 245; MMD autobiography fragment, 1948.

35. The author found the one-page typescript at the DMA in a box labeled "to decide later date." The fragment is labeled "P 11, Bk 2," suggesting that it comes from Marie's autobiography. The paragraph containing the quoted passage begins by saying, "Looking back over the 18 years—first the struggle of getting Lee's bills paid, saving for our house—then the depression and our poverty days," which indicates that the passage was written in about 1948, after eighteen years of marriage.

36. MMD interview; Eickman, "Love just like in the movies"; "Where Were You?" film no. FCA 1595, Motion Picture Division, Library of Congress.

37. LD, *Father,* 411; Lubell, "Magnificent Failure," January 31: 48; Los Angeles *Times,* 10 November 1952: pt. 4, 1.

38. See, for example, Marilyn to LD, 20 March 1944, box 1940 (2); Eleanor to LD, 30 September 1947, box 1940 (3); Harriet to LD, 30 August 1953, box 1950 (2), all in DMA. Harriet, following the Stanton-Blatch tradition of female liberation, was a professional painter and a flight instructor (she trained Navy pilots during World War II). Cf. LD, *Father,* 460–62.

39. Rhoda Jenkins interview; LD to Harry Maizlish, 22 July 1958, folder Personal, January–July 1958, DMA.

40. Marilyn to LD, 11 March 1936, box 1930 (2), DMA; LD to Charles de Forest, 1 June 1931, ct. 1, LDP; Glen Behymer to LD, 14 September 1951, and LD to Behymer, 18 September 1951, personal correspondence, DMA; undated and unidentified clippings in box 11, De Forest Family Papers.

41. Carneal, *Conqueror,* 295; MMD interview.

42. William H. Pouch to LD, 20 February 1951, box 1950 (1), DMA; LD to David C. Fenner, 26 February 1957; LD to American Red Cross Emergency Fund, 7 August 1951; LD to Save the Children Foundation, 14 January 1952; LD to George Sloan, 8 April 1953; canceled check dated 24 December 1954, and made out to Mount Hermon, all in personal correspondence, DMA; MMD interview.

43. New York *Times,* 9 January 1930: 22; copy of script in box 1930 (2), DMA; World's Fair brochure in ct. 2, LDP; *Electrical Engineering* 66, no. 3 (March 1947): 254; LD, *Father,* 459; *The Talladegan* 68, no. 7 (June 1951): n.p.; New York *Times,* 9 April 1952: 33; mimeographed history of De Forest Pioneers accompanying Joel J. Michaels to Librarian of Yale, 27 August 1956, box 12, De Forest Family Papers; Irving E. Levine, *Electronics Pioneer: Lee De Forest* (New York: Julian Messner, 1964), 183; LD to Ralph Edwards, 7 June 1957, "This Is Your Life" correspondence, DMA; dedication program in box 1950 (3), DMA.

44. Undated note by MMD, box labeled "decide later," DMA; MMD interview.

45. Omaha *World Herald Magazine,* 2 April 1950: 6-C; LD to Annabel Lee, 2 December 1952, and LD to Edna Robb Webster, 11 May 1953, both in personal correspondence, DMA; W. L. Marxer to Whom It May Concern, 1 December 1953, box 1950 (2), DMA; LD's secretary to Eloise McCaskill, 15 March 1955, McCaskill correspondence, DMA; Joel J. Michaels to E. J. Simon, 10 February 1958, De Forest Pioneers Memorabilia, Emil Simon Autobiography, Bancroft Library, University of California, Berkeley; AP wirecopy, datelined Hollywood, 26 August [1957], box 1950 (3), DMA.

Chapter 7: *Father of Radio:* 1950

1. LD to D. J. Johnson, 14 October 1953, Correspondence File 1955–56 [sic], DMA.

2. LD, "Fragmentary Study in Autobiography"; "Diaries"; "Father of Radio"; LD, *Father.*

3. LD to —, 30 March 1949, Journal 23.

4. LD, *Father,* vii.

5. LD to Samuel Lubell, 25 September 1950, autobiography correspondence, DMA; LD, *Father,* vii, 466.

6. LD, *Father,* 45; Henry De Forest to LD, n.d., Journal 3; 8 June 1891, Journal 1; 18 June 1899, Journal 14; 31 May 1907, Journal 18; 28 January 1920, Journal 20.

7. Carneal, *Conqueror,* 67–68; W. E. Henley, *Poems,* vol. 1 (London: David Nutt, 1908), 125; LD, *Father,* 465. In 1906 LD said he wished he could be "master of my soul" (19 July 1906, Journal 17).

8. White to LD, 26 August 1905, and LD to White, 28 August 1905, in scrapbook.

9. *Father,* 138, 358, 464–465.

10. Calendar for 1897, ct. 2, LDP; 14 March 1897, Journal 11; ca. 4 August 1897, Journal 12.

11. LD, *Father,* 289, 413. For dating of the poem, see 6 February 1921 [sic], Journal 21.

12. 11 April 1897, Journal 11.

13. LD to Arthur S. Ford, 10 March 1930, box 1930 (1), DMA. See also LD, *Television,* 93–94.

14. Josephson, *Edison,* 155; Helen M. Fessenden, *Fessenden* (New York: Coward-McCann, 1940), 202–3, 272, 275–85; Pupin, *From Immigrant to Inventor,* 341, 366–78, 383–87.

15. Maclaurin, *Invention and Innovation,* 245, 247; Tyne, *Saga of the Vacuum Tube,* 86. See also Jewkes, Sawers, and Stillerman, *Sources of Invention,* 103, and Norbert Wiener, *The Human Use of Human Beings,* 2nd ed. (Boston: Houghton Mifflin, 1954), 113–15. To use Wiener's Dickensian terminology, de Forest was one

of the last Doyces in a world managed by the Mudfog Association.

16. Leonard S. Reich, *The Making of American Industrial Research* (Cambridge: Cambridge University Press, 1985), 3–4; Hughes, *American Genesis,* 15, 138, 183.

17. LD to Charles de Forest, 18 October 1931, ct. 1, LDP. See also New York *Times,* 15 November 1931: sec. 9, p. 8.

18. LD, *Father,* vii, 4.

19. Dust jacket in box 11, De Forest Family Papers; LD, *Father,* 3–4.

20. Tyne, *Saga of the Vacuum Tube,* 41–42, 90; Aitken, *Continuous Wave,* 231, 244, 548, 550.

21. Lessing, *Man of High Fidelity,* 309, lists seven basic inventions in the history of radio, of which only two might be attributed to LD.

22. Maclaurin, *Invention and Innovation,* 43–44, 247.

23. Ibid., 11–21, 58; Archer, *History of Radio,* 53–55; Hugh G. J. Aitken, *Syntony and Spark—the Origins of Radio* (New York: Wiley & Sons, 1976), 27.

24. 11 May 1920, Journal 20.

25. 25 January 1891, Journal 1; 1 February 1897, Journal 11; 26 June 1906, Journal 17.

26. 6 May 1891, Journal 1; 13 and 16 March 1911, "Leaves from Diary"; 19 July 1919, Journal 19; 2 May 1920, Journal 20. LD never perceived any contradiction between biological determinism and willful individualism.

27. "Leaves from Diary," pp. 4–5; 1 June 1923, Journal 21; LD to Anna De Forest, Nov. [n.d.] 1924, ct. 1, LDP.

28. Undated clipping from the *Congregationalist,* in scrapbook. An early example of his calling himself Father of Broadcasting is his diary entry for 13 January 1924, Journal 22. A booklet published by the De Forest Radio Co. in 1928 is titled "Helpful Hints for Better Radio by Dr. Lee de Forest, 'The Father of Radio' " (De Forest Memorabilia, Emil Jacob Simon Autobiography, Bancroft Library, University of California, Berkeley). In 1956 he claimed to be "father of electronics" ("New Frontiers," MS dated 26 March 1956, box 1950 [3], DMA). LD re-read his journals as early as 6 September 1891 (Journal 2) and as late as when he was working on *Father* (which freely quotes from them). For an example of retrospection during the time when he began to call himself father of radio, see 7 September 1925, Journal 22.

29. Ts by MMD, dated 28 August 1952, box labeled "decide later," DMA; Jane Morgan, *Electronics in the West* (Palo Alto: National Press Books, 1967), 46.

30. LD, *Father,* 138–40, 194, 287.

31. Unidentified clipping in box ND (2), DMA.

32. 10 August 1906, Journal 17; LD, *Father,* 320.

33. 17 May 1925, Journal 22; 26 December 1926, Journal 23; 5 January 1945, box 1940 (2), DMA.

34. Archer, *History of Radio;* Warren C. Scoville [?] to LD, 3 August 1945, and Ts by Maclaurin in box 1940 (2), DMA; LD to Jerene Claire Cline, 18 June 1951, Cline correspondence, DMA; *Newsweek,* 11 June 1951: 60–63; Lewis, *Empire of the Air,* 338. LD's reputation would not burgeon after his death. In 1991, when Oxford University Press planned a twenty-volume series, *American National Biography,* listing many thousands of "figures who played significant roles in American history," the editors were undecided whether LD deserved to be included. Cf. Sara E. Lawrence to author, 22 March and 10 July 1991.

35. LD to W. J. Barkley, 16 April 1929, and LD to James W. Garside, 13 May 1929, both in De Forest Radio Co. Correspondence, box 41, Clark Collection; LD to Mary Ralph, 10 January [n.y.], box 1930 (1), DMA; LD to Frank Butler, 5

January 1945, box 1940 (2), DMA.

36. Autobiography, Cline, and personal correspondence, DMA; LD to Jessica Wallace Millar, postmarked 16 July 1951, box 11, De Forest Family Papers.

37. Harry Maizlish to LD, 25 September 1957, box 1950 (3); LD to Jerene Claire Cline, 26 April 1951, Cline correspondence; Cline to Rep. Patrick J. Hillings, 11 May 1951, and Cline to Hopper, 18 May 1951, Cline correspondence, all in DMA.

38. LD to E. J. Simon, 15 August 1952, personal correspondence; Lewis, *Empire of the Air,* 340; Gernsback to LD, 28 December 1954; LD to Gernsback, 30 December; LD to Gernsback, 16 May 1955, Nobel correspondence; box 1950 (2), all in DMA; Gernsback to Lawrence, 22 April 1955, and Lawrence to Gernsback, 26 April 1955, carton 6, folder 15, Lawrence Papers, Bancroft Library, University of California, Berkeley; *Radio-Electronics,* March 1955: 31.

39. LD to Eugenia H. Farrar, 21 February 1955, autobiography correspondence; LD to Gernsback, 14 November 1955, Gernsback correspondence; LD to Gernsback, 28 February and 9 May 1955, Nobel correspondence, all in DMA.

40. New York *Times,* 21 July 1937: 14; LD, *Father,* 457.

41. 15 January 1920, Journal 20; Lessing, *Man of High Fidelity,* 299; *Scientific American,* July 1954: 2; LD to Carl Dreher, 15 May 1956, box 1950 (3), DMA.

42. MMD interview; Joel Michaels to E. J. Simons, 23 February 1960, in De Forest Pioneers Memorabilia, Simon Autobiography.

43. LD to David C. Mearns, 1 December 1954, autobiography correspondence; Alton H. Keller to LD, 19 September 1955, box 1950 (2); deed of gift, dated 9 November 1955, Library of Congress correspondence; Jane Morgan to Ralph Heintz, 20 October 1966, all in DMA; telephone conversation between the author and George Durfey, accession chairman of the Perham Foundation, 13 November 1991.

44. Obituaries from *Radio-Electronics,* September 1961, and *Electronic News,* 28 August 1961, both in De Forest Memorabilia, Simon Autobiography; Emil Simon to Raymond Guy, 8 February 1960; De Forest Pioneers memo, 20 April 1962; Raymond Guy to directors of De Forest Pioneers, 30 March 1960; and memo from Lloyd Espenschied, 24 February 1960, all in De Forest Pioneers Memorabilia, Simon Autobiography.

45. Unidentified clipping, ca. 1 July 1961, box 11, De Forest Family Papers. Marie Mosquini de Forest continued living in Hollywood until 1967, when she moved to Hemet, California. In 1984 she was moved to a nursing home in Los Angeles, where she died in obscurity in about 1987. Cf. Lewis, *Empire of the Air,* 343.

Sources Consulted

Unpublished Sources: Archives, Manuscripts, Dissertations, Interviews, and Films

Case, Theodore W., Archives. The Cayuga Museum. Auburn, N.Y.

Clark, George, Collection. National Museum of American History, Smithsonian Institution, Washington, D.C.

De Forest Family Papers. Manuscripts and Archives Division, Yale University Library, New Haven, Conn.

De Forest, Lee, Memorial Archives (DMA). Electronics Museum of the Perham Foundation, Los Altos, Calif. The DMA contains correspondence, notes, sketches, manuscripts, photographs, clippings, miscellaneous items, and a scrapbook containing various important documents. When this book was in press, the Electronics Museum had left Foothill College in Los Altos Hills, Calif., and was looking for a new home.

De Forest, Lee, Papers (LDP). Manuscript Division, Library of Congress, Washington, D.C. The 23 journals that LD kept between 1893 and 1949 comprise the bulk of the LDP. The collection also includes letters, notes, sketches, photographs, clippings, printed matter, and miscellaneous items.

De Forest, Lee. "Autobiographical Notes." 6 "volumes" (folders), 1939. TMs in DMA.

———. "The Diaries of Doctor De Forest." 2 vols. 1939. TMs in box 12, De Forest Family Papers.

———. "Father of Radio: The Autobiography of Lee de Forest." 1948. TMs in De Forest Family Papers. This is longer and much cruder than the published autobiography.

———. "A Fragmentary Study in Autobiography Written in 1902–03." TMs in box 1900 (1), DMA.

———. Journals 1–23. In LDP.

———. "Leaves from the Diary of a Baby, Harriot Stanton de Forest. As I find her after six months absence in California." TMs, March 1911, in box 1900 (2), DMA.

———. "Scientific Oration." 1893. TMs in box 2, LDP.

———. Scrapbook. In DMA.

———. Statistical Questions. A questionnaire distributed to seniors in the Sheffield Scientific School, class of 1896, and filled out by LD. In box 2, LDP.

De Forest, Marie Mosquini. Interview with author. Hemet, Calif., 21 January 1975.

Douglas, Susan Jeanne. "Exploring Pathways in the Ether: The Formative Years of Radio in America, 1896–1912." Ph.D. diss., Brown University, 1980.

Espenschied, Lloyd, Reminiscences of. 1963. Oral History Collection of Columbia University, New York.

Hijiya, James A. "The De Forests: Three American Lives." Ph.D. diss., Cornell University, 1977.

Jenkins, Rhoda Barney. Interview with author. Greenwich, Conn., 23 February 1991.

————. Photograph collection at her home in Greenwich. Many photos and some documents pertaining to the woman suffrage movement.

Kingsley, William L., Memorial Collection. Manuscripts and Archives Division, Yale University Library, New Haven, Conn.

Lawrence, Ernest O., Papers. Bancroft Library, University of California, Berkeley.

Seifer, Marc. J. "Nikola Tesla: Psychohistory of a Forgotten Inventor." Ph.D. diss., Saybrook Institute (San Francisco), 1987.

Simon, Emil, Autobiography. Bancroft Library, University of California, Berkeley.

Woolsey Family Papers. Manuscript and Archives Division, Yale University Library, New Haven, Conn.

Zouary, Maurice, Collection. Phonofilms made by LD. In Motion Picture, Broadcasting and Recorded Sound Division, Library of Congress, Washington, D.C.

————. "First Sound of Movies." Photocopy of MS. 1976. In Motion Picture Reading Room, Library of Congress.

Published Sources: Books and Articles

Aitken, Hugh G. J. *The Continuous Wave: Technology and American Radio, 1900–1932*. Princeton: Princeton University Press, 1985.

————. *Syntony and Spark—the Origins of Radio*. New York: John Wiley & Sons, 1976.

Anderson, James D. *The Education of Blacks in the South, 1860–1935*. Chapel Hill: University of North Carolina Press, 1988.

Archer, Gleason. *History of Radio to 1926*. New York: American Historical Society, 1938.

Arvin, Newton. *Longfellow: His Life and Work*. Boston: Little, Brown, 1963.

Barnhart, Robert K., ed. *The Barnhart Dictionary of Etymology*. N.p.: H. W. Wilson Co., 1988.

Barnouw, Erik. *A Tower in Babel: A History of Broadcasting in the United States*, vol. 1. New York: Oxford University Press, 1966.

Basalla, George. *The Evolution of Technology*. Cambridge: Cambridge University Press, 1988.

Bazin, Andre. "The Myth of Total Cinema." In *What Is Cinema?*, tran. Hugh Gray. Berkeley: University of California Press, 1967.

Bond, Horace Mann. *Social and Economic Influences on the Public Education of Negroes in Alabama, 1865–1930*. Washington, D.C.: Associated Publishers, 1939.

Bridges, William E. "Warm Hearth, Cold World: Social Perspectives on the Household Poets." *American Quarterly* 2, no. 4 (Winter 1969): 764–79.

Bruce, Robert V. *Bell: Alexander Graham Bell and the Conquest of Solitude.* Boston: Little, Brown, 1973.

Butchart, Ronald E. *Northern Schools, Southern Blacks, and Reconstruction.* Westport, Conn.: Greenwood, 1980.

Butler, Addie L. J. *The Distinctive Black College: Talladega, Tuskegee, and Morehouse.* Metuchen, N.J.: Scarecrow, 1977.

Carneal, Georgette. *A Conqueror of Space: An Authorized Biography of the Life and Work of Lee De Forest.* New York: Horace Liveright, 1930.

Cashdollar, Charles D. *The Transformation of Theology, 1830–1890: Positivism and Protestant Thought in Britain and America.* Princeton: Princeton University Press, 1989.

Cheney, Margaret. *Tesla: Man Out of Time.* New York: Dorset, 1989.

Chipman, Robert A. "De Forest and the Triode Detector." *Scientific American* 212 (March 1965): 92–100.

Clark, George H. *The Life of John Stone Stone: Mathematician, Physicist, Electrical Engineer and Great Inventor.* San Diego: Frye & Smith, 1946.

Cooper, Bryant S. *The Philosophy of Sir Oliver Lodge.* Nashville: Vanderbilt University Press, 1934.

Danielian, N. R. *A.T.&T.: The Story of Industrial Conquest.* New York: Vanguard, 1939.

De Forest, Lee. "The Audion, A New Receiver for Wireless Telegraphy." *Transactions of the American Institute of Electrical Engineers* 25 (1907): 735–63.

———. *Father of Radio: The Autobiography of Lee de Forest.* Chicago: Wilcox & Follett, 1950.

———. "The Motion Picture Speaks." *Popular Radio* 3, no. 3 (March 1923): 159–69.

———. "The Phonofilm." *Transactions of the Society of Motion Picture Engineers* 16 (May 1923): 61–75.

———. "Phonofilm Progress." *Transactions of the Society of Motion Picture Engineers,* no. 20 (September–October 1924): 17–19.

———. "The Progress in Aerial Navigation." *Yale Scientific Monthly* 2, no. 2 (November 1895): 53–67.

———. "Progress in Aerial Navigation—1934." *Yale Scientific Magazine* 9, no. 1 (Fall 1934): 3–5, 21–22.

———. "Progress of Radio-Telephony." *Electrical World* 53, no. 1 (2 January 1909): 13.

———. "Recent Developments in 'The Phonofilm.'" *Transactions of the Society of Motion Picture Engineers,* no. 27 (October 1926): 64–76.

———. "Recent Developments in the Work of the Federal Telegraph Co." *Proceedings of the Institute of Radio Engineers* 1 (January 1917); repr. *Proceedings of the Institute of Electrical and Electronics Engineers* 51, no. 3 (March 1963): 426–33.

———. "Reflection of Hertzian Waves at the Ends of Parallel Wires." Ph.D. diss., Yale University, 1899. Published in *American Journal of Science,* 4th ser., 8, no. 43 (July 1899): 58–71.

———. *Television: Today and Tomorrow.* New York: Dial, 1942.

———. *Wireless in the Home.* New York: De Forest Radio Telephone & Telegraph, 1922.

Dictionary of Scientific Biography, vol. 4, ed. Charles Coulston Gillispie. New York: Scribner's Sons, 1971. S.v. "Lee de Forest," by Charles Süsskind.

Douglas, Susan. *Inventing American Broadcasting 1899–1922*. Baltimore: Johns Hopkins University Press, 1987.

DuBois, Ellen, ed. "Spanning Two Centuries: The Autobiography of Nora Stanton Barney." *History Workshop Journal* no. 22 (Fall 1986): 131–52.

Dunlap, Orrin E. Jr. *Marconi: The Man and His Wireless*. New York: Macmillan, 1937.

———. *Radio's 100 Men of Science*. New York: Harper & Bros., 1944.

Eickman, Pat. "Love just like in the movies." Riverside, Calif. *Press*, 19 October 1972: C-1

Fessenden, Helen M. *Fessenden: Builder of Tomorrows*. New York: Coward-McCann, 1940.

Fleming, J. Ambrose. *Memories of a Scientific Life*. London: Marshall, Morgan & Scott, 1934.

———. *The Thermionic Valve and Its Developments in Radio-Telegraphy and Telephony*. London: Wireless Press, 1924.

Henley, William Ernest. *Poems*, vol. 1. London: David Nutt, 1908.

Hofstadter, Richard. *Social Darwinism in American Thought*, rev. ed. Boston: Beacon, 1955.

Howeth, L. S. *History of Communications-Electronics in the United States Navy*. Washington: Government Printing Office, 1963.

Hughes, Thomas P. *American Genesis: A Century of Invention and Technological Enthusiasm 1870–1970*. New York: Viking, 1989.

Hunt, Inez, and Wanetta W. Draper. *Lightning in His Hand: The Life Story of Nikola Tesla*. Hawthorne, Calif.: Omni Publications, 1964.

Jewkes, John, David Sawers, and Richard Stillerman. *The Sources of Invention*, 2nd ed. New York: Norton, 1969.

Jolly, W. P. *Marconi*. New York: Stein & Day, 1972.

———. *Sir Oliver Lodge*. Rutherford, N.J.: Fairleigh Dickinson Press, 1974.

Jones, Maxine D., and Joe M. Richardson. *Talladega College: The First Century*. Tuscaloosa: University of Alabama Press, 1990.

Josephson, Matthew. *Edison*. New York: McGraw-Hill, 1959.

Kellogg, Edward W. "History of Sound Motion Pictures." *Journal of the Society of Motion Picture and Television Engineers* 64 (June–August 1955). Repr. in Raymond Fielding, ed., *A Technological History of Motion Pictures and Television*. Berkeley: University of California Press, 1967: 174–220.

Knapp, R. H., and H. B. Goodrich. *Origins of American Scientists*. Chicago: University of Chicago, 1952.

Kreuger, Miles. "The Birth of the American Film Musical." *High Fidelity* (July 1972): 42–48.

Lessing, Lawrence. *Man of High Fidelity: Edwin Howard Armstrong*. Philadelphia: Lippincott, 1956.

Levine, Irving Englander. *Electronics Pioneer: Lee De Forest*. New York: Julian Messner, 1964.

Levine, Lawrence W. *Defender of the Faith: William Jennings Bryan: The Last Decade 1915–1924*. New York: Oxford University Press, 1965.

Lewis, Tom. *Empire of the Air: The Men Who Made Radio.* New York: Harper Collins, 1991.

Lodge, Oliver. *Past Years: An Autobiography.* London: Hodder & Stoughton, 1931.

———. *Phantom Walls.* New York: Putnam's Sons, 1930.

Longfellow, Henry Wadsworth. *Poetical Works,* vol. 1. Boston: Houghton-Mifflin, 1893.

Lubell, Samuel. "Magnificent Failure." *Saturday Evening Post,* 17 January 1942: 9–80 passim; 24 January: 20–43 passim; 31 January: 27–49 passim.

Mabee, Carleton. *The American Leonardo: A Life of Samuel F. B. Morse.* New York: Knopf, 1943.

Macgowan, Kenneth. *Behind the Screen: The History and Techniques of the Motion Picture.* New York: Delacorte, 1965.

MacGregor-Morris, J. T. *The Invention of the Valve: A Biography of Sir Ambrose Fleming.* London: The Television Society, 1954.

Maclaurin, W. Rupert. *Invention and Innovation in the Radio Industry.* New York: Macmillan, 1949.

McLean, A. S. "De Forest System of Wireless Telegraphy." *Yale Scientific Monthly* 10, no. 1 (October 1903): 3–9.

Marconi, Degna. *My Father, Marconi.* New York: McGraw Hill, 1962.

Marconi Wireless Telegraph Co. of America v. United States, 320 U.S. 1. In *United States Reports* 320 (Washington: Government Printing Office, 1944), 1–80.

Marvin, Carolyn. *When Old Technologies Were New: Thinking About Electric Communication in the Late Nineteenth Century.* New York: Oxford University Press, 1988.

Miessner, Benjamin Franklin. *On the Early History of Radio Guidance.* San Francisco: San Francisco Press, 1964.

Moore, R. Laurence. *In Search of White Crows: Spiritualism, Parapsychology, and American Culture.* New York: Oxford University Press, 1977.

Morgan, Jane. *Electronics in the West: The First Fifty Years.* Palo Alto, Calif.: National Press Books, 1967.

National Cyclopaedia of American Biography. New York: James T. White. Vol. A (1930). S. v. "Lee de Forest": 18–19

———. Vol. 35 (1949). S.v. "Henry Swift De Forest": 337.

———. Vol. 37 (1951). S.v. "Charles Mills de Forest": 190.

New York *Times,* 1906–1952

Noble, David. *America by Design: Science, Technology, and the Rise of Corporate Capitalism.* New York: Knopf, 1977.

"The Officers of the American De Forest Wireless Telegraph Company." *Wireless Age* 1, no. 2 (March 1905): 11–15.

O'Neill, John J. *Prodigal Genius: The Life of Nikola Tesla.* New York: Ives Washburn, 1944.

Pauly, Philip J. *Controlling Life: Jacques Loeb and the Engineering Ideal in Biology.* New York: Oxford University Press, 1987.

Poe, Edgar Allan. "Eleonora," in *The Complete Works of Edgar Allan Poe,* ed. James A. Harrison, vol. 4. New York: AMS Press, 1965, 236–44.

———. "Mesmeric Revelation," in *Complete Works,* 5: 241–54.

Pupin, Michael. *From Immigrant to Inventor.* New York: Scribner's Sons, 1924.

Reich, Leonard S. *The Making of American Industrial Research: Science and Business at GE and Bell, 1876–1926.* Cambridge: Cambridge University Press, 1985.

——. "Research, Patents, and the Struggle to Control Radio: A Study of Big Business and the Uses of Industrial Research." *Business History Review* 51, no. 2 (Summer 1977): 208–35.

Richardson, Joe M. *Christian Reconstruction: The American Missionary Association and Southern Blacks, 1861–1890.* Athens: University of Georgia Press, 1986.

Rockefeller, Terry Kay. "BARNEY, Nora Stanton Blatch." In *Notable American Women: The Modern Period,* vol. 1, Barbara Sicherman and Carol Hurd Green et al., eds. Cambridge: Harvard University Press, 1980: 53–55.

Roe, Anne. "A Psychologist Examines 64 Eminent Scientists." *Scientific American* 187, no. 5 (November 1952): 21–25.

Rosenfeld, Albert. *The Quintessence of Irving Langmuir: A Biography.* In *The Collected Works of Irving Langmuir,* vol. 12, C. Guy Suits, ed. New York: Pergamon, 1962: 1–229.

Segal, Howard P. *Technological Utopianism in American Culture.* Chicago: University of Chicago Press, 1985.

Sherer, Robert G. *Subordination or Liberation? The Development and Conflicting Theories of Black Education in Nineteenth Century Alabama.* University, Ala.: University of Alabama Press, 1977.

Sherry, Michael S. *The Rise of American Air Power: The Creation of Armageddon.* New Haven: Yale University Press, 1987.

Shiers, George. *Bibliography of the History of Electronics.* Metuchen, N.J.: Scarecrow Press, 1972.

——. "The First Electron Tube." *Scientific American* 220 (March 1969): 104–12.

Statistics of the Population of the United States at the Tenth Census (June 1, 1880), vol. 1. Washington: Government Printing Office, 1883.

The Students' Idea (Talladega College), vol. 5, no. 5 (April 1904). Special issue in memoriam of Henry Swift De Forest.

Swint, Henry L. *The Northern Teacher in the South 1862–1870.* New York: Octagon, 1967.

Tartakoff, Helen H. "The Normal Personality in Our Culture and the Nobel Prize Complex." In *Psychoanalysis—A General Psychology: Essays in Honor of Heinz Hartmann,* Rudolph Loewenstein et àl., eds. New York: International Universities Press, 1966: 222–52.

Tennyson, Alfred Lord. *The Poetic and Dramatic Works of Alfred Lord Tennyson.* Boston: Houghton Mifflin, 1898.

Tesla, Nikola. *My Inventions: The Autobiography of Nikola Tesla,* ed. Ben Johnston. Williston, VT: Hart Bros, 1982. Consists of six articles that originally appeared in *Electrical Experimenter* magazine in 1919.

Turner, James. *Without God, Without Creed: The Origins of Unbelief in America.* Baltimore: Johns Hopkins University Press, 1985.

Tyne, Gerald F. J. *Saga of the Vacuum Tube.* Indianapolis: Howard W. Sams, 1977.

Udelson, Joseph H. *The Great Television Race: A History of the American Television Industry 1925–1941.* University, Ala.: University of Alabama Press, 1982.

Wade, Herbert T. "Wireless Telegraphy by the De Forest System." *Review of Reviews* 35 (June 1907): 681–85.

Wasserman, Neil H. *From Invention to Innovation: Long-Distance Telephone Transmission at the Turn of the Century.* Baltimore: Johns Hopkins University Press, 1985.

Wiener, Norbert. *The Human Uses of Human Beings,* 2nd ed. Boston: Houghton-Mifflin, 1954.

Zouary, Maurice H. *The Great Brain Robbery of Scientist, Dr. Lee De Forest.* Pamphlet in Lee de Forest folder, Motion Picture Reading Room, Library of Congress, Washington, D.C.

Index